Primary Mathematics Curriculum Guide

HARVEY BLAIR and PAT HUGHES

David Fulton Publishers
London

David Fulton Publishers Ltd
Ormond House, 26–27 Boswell Street, London WC1N 3JZ

www.fultonpublishers.co.uk

First published in Great Britain by David Fulton Publishers 2001

British Library Cataloguing in Publication Data
A catalogue record for this book is available from the British Library

ISBN 1-85346-812-6

The publishers would like to thank Sophie Cox and Sheila Harding for proofreading this book.

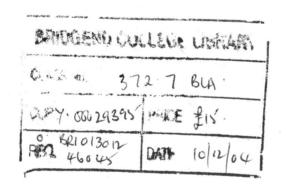
Typeset by Elite Typesetting Techniques, Eastleigh, Hampshire
Printed in Great Britain by Bell and Bain Ltd, Glasgow

Contents

Preface

This Study Guide forms part of the distance learning package produced for the part-time primary PGCE course at Liverpool Hope University College. The guide has been piloted by two groups of students and updated in line with additional materials and ideas from the National Numeracy Team. We are also indebted to schools who have allowed us to use their planning guides as exemplars. The guide has been written by primary practitioners who are also professional writers. A deliberate attempt has been made to capture the ethos of the taught courses and to provide readers with lively, interactive texts. For this reason, it is likely that other trainee teachers, student mentors in school, subject coordinators and teacher trainers will find the materials useful. Space has been left within the text for readers to write in their comments and findings. Some may prefer to keep a separate history file for this. Keeping a file also means that it is possible to add additional information from other readings to build up personal resources to acompany this guide.

Government initiatives which are pertinent to the material in the guides are available through the Government websites, such as the DfEE standards site at www.standards. dfee.gov.uk

Harvey Blair and Pat Hughes
June 2001

Acknowledgements

Our sincere thanks to:

Liz Fleet	Balacotier P.S. (Isle of Man)
Tony Fleet	Prescot C.P. (Knowsley LEA)
Gillian Fassioms	Longview C.P. (Knowsley LEA)
Norman Jones	

and to the Distance Learners of 1999 and 2000 for their comments and suggestions on the first version of this book.

Chapter 1

Introducting the book's objectives

By the end of this chapter you will have:
- gained an understanding of how to proceed through this curriculum guide;
- discovered how to respond to and reflect on set tasks and activities, including making reference to your school's mathematics policy documents, statements and practice;
- made some progress in identifying and articulating your beliefs about mathematics;
- been introduced to some issues in the teaching and learning of mathematics;
- learned to appreciate some of the many resources available for teaching and learning maths;
- been introduced to key texts for undertaking the government Skills Test in Numeracy.

Using the book

In any distance-learning course, predominantly based on the printed word, it is not possible to emulate precisely the cut-and-thrust of the classroom debate of a traditional PGCE course. Therefore this book is structured around a range of tasks. You may be required to work with a prescribed text and the instruction 'Read' should be viewed as shorthand for 'read, make notes and carry out suggested activities' or to carry out an activity with children, adults (usually teachers) or on yourself.

Your interaction will take a variety of forms but will generally involve you in making some written response about the outcomes. You will then be expected to compare your thoughts with the commentary provided (as well as with your mentor and other students as you begin to set up support networks). Some commentary usually follows each task and may encourage you to make further, more detailed notes. You therefore need to create a file in which to collect your responses.

One final point – although you are expected, as far as possible, to tackle every task, you may have to modify a few individual tasks to fit your circumstances.

The chapters

Each chapter begins with a list of objectives (see above). These are to help you to:
- focus your learning;
- assess the extent to which you have achieved these through the work in the sections, and decide whether further work is necessary.

Begin by working through the **first three chapters.** These will give you an overview of the aims of the book, the implications of the maths National Curriculum itself, and an understanding of the National Numeracy Framework (NNF).

The National Numeracy Strategy

The first draft of this maths guide was developed at the same time as *The National Numeracy Strategy: Framework for teaching mathematics from Reception to Year 6* (NNS or NNF) (DfEE 1999a) was sent into all schools. Chapter 3 looks at this in more detail and it is assumed that all students will have their own copy of the Framework and be familiar with its content. Additional DfEE materials are available in schools from the subject coordinator.

The role of any curriculum mathematics course is to explore the nature of mathematics and its teaching and learning in much greater detail. Trainee teachers are at the start of learning to be teachers. The NNF has been written for experienced teachers.

Teaching maths

The following text and tasks aim to help you identify your own perception of what mathematics and the teaching of it mean to you. This chapter also touches briefly on issues such as numeracy, multicultural maths, calculators and commercial maths schemes. These should raise and heighten your awareness and help you to locate and develop your own ideas. Each of these issues and more will be developed in later chapters.

Your own opinion on maths

You will already have a wealth of experience of maths teaching and learning, both as a pupil yourself and also through the perceptions of others, perhaps family members and the media. You may also have spent some recent classroom time as a teacher's aide. Whatever your experience you will have formed impressions, even opinions, about what constitutes good and effective maths teaching.

Task 1

Begin your file with a mathematical 'autobiography' by noting initial thoughts about your own learning of mathematics. You should add to these as you progress through the book whenever further memories occur to you. It is worth dating each entry and leaving space to add other appropriate thoughts and ideas that come to you.

What are your beliefs about teaching mathematics and where do they come from? Reflect on, and make an initial note of, your own experiences of learning mathematics, especially as a child. Were these positive or negative? Do your recollections generate powerful emotional responses? What reasons can you give for this?

You are likely, as this book is intended for primary PGCE students, to have considered your own primary experience and whether you identified yourself or were identified as being successful or otherwise in maths.

Reasons you may have given for liking or disliking maths might include:
- finding the subject easy or difficult;
- relationships with teachers, parents or peers;
- the teaching style and classroom organisation;
- connotations (especially social) with images of maths;
- the language used to communicate the subject.

Task 2

If you haven't already done so, compare and contrast your primary school maths experience with that of your secondary school years. How did they differ and how do you account for these differences?

By the end of the primary years, many children will have formed attitudes to maths which, especially if negative, may be difficult to change. For some, their success at primary school, which was based on their ability to perform standard written calculations, may be tempered or even negated as they meet the more abstract aspects of the subject. Conversely, some adults report that 'things began to fall into place', perhaps as the result of some inspirational or sympathetic teaching.

 ## What is maths?

In a very powerful sense 'maths is all around us'. It is used in everyday life – in the home, at work, during leisure activities, as well as in other school subjects. People are often surprised when this 'hidden' aspect of maths is pointed out to them, sometimes so much so that they will say it isn't 'real' like the maths they learned in school. For example, studies of 10- to 12-year-old Brazilian street children have shown that while they could mentally calculate and recalculate with large numbers (and simultaneously monitor an inflation rate of about 250% at the time) they were unable to perform accurately the standard, simple written arithmetic taught in school. Similarly, a clerk in this country had been shown how to calculate the VAT at 17.5% on VAT-inclusive prices by simply multiplying the price by 0.851 and rounding to the nearest penny, using a calculator of course! This was performed confidently and successfully time and again. When asked, the clerk had no idea why the process worked and commented that 'We didn't do this when I was at school'.

This anecdote shows clearly that for many people maths is only about what you do at school, quite often alone and in silence, usually with pencil and paper, applying well-defined sets of procedures and rules, and having little relevance to themselves apart from a basic arithmetic function. (A child who was asked what she did at school that day replied that: 'I learned a poem in English, found out about the Romans building walls in Britain, measured how much my plant had grown in science, and did pages 14 and 15 in maths'!)

(Note: pp. 60 and 61 in *The National Curriculum 2000* (DfEE/QCA 1999) make useful reading.)

 ## Ways of calculating

There is often an inability to link maths to everyday life. To combat this and to help children use methods of calculation which are most appropriate to a given context and to their own level of confidence, the National Numeracy Strategy makes overt, and legitimises by government policy, the use of *ad hoc* and infrequently-taught mental methods of calculation. In daily one-hour sessions children's own methods are to be valued, made explicit, discussed and practised. Where appropriate, children will be taught techniques such as doubling, and decomposing and recomposing numbers, to aid calculation. It is expected that the value of maths done in the home will gain a higher profile as adults become involved in the underlying principles of the NNS.

Task 3

Perform these calculations in your usual way:

5 + 9	139 + 28	3964 + 7123 + 4918 + 5960
13 – 8	85 – 20	592 – 276
4 x 7	17 x 3	931 x 768
35 ÷ 5	72 ÷ 4	8391 ÷ 57

Identify the strategies you used. For which calculations did you use a mental approach only; a written method; a combination of written and mental; a calculator?
It is clearly beneficial for children to have instant recall of as many facts as possible, but they also need to have a range of strategies, especially mental, to 'figure out' those that do not immediately come to mind.

The use of calculators

> It seems paradoxical that using a calculator in maths lessons is often seen as cheating, while the use of ICT (Information and Communications Technology) is generally welcomed as beneficial! Many people do not appreciate the potential of the calculator as a pedagogical or teaching device which helps children to understand the structure of our number system. Calculators can also be used to explore rapidly-generated number patterns and enable children to work with realistic data in solving problems.

Task 4

Consider the contentious role of the calculator in learning mathematics. When, if at all, should children use one? Write down your thoughts on the rights and wrongs of using a calculator in maths lessons. Are you for or against them, or in favour of just occasional use? Justify your stance. What guidance does the NNF give?

How do children learn maths and what is the best way to teach it?

> Let's move now to ideas about maths learning and approaches to classroom organisation. Other parts of the book will introduce you in more detail to those theories, mainly from different branches of psychology, which have been influential in shaping classroom practice. You should never forget that no one theory alone adequately describes how children learn in every case and that 'fitness for purpose' must be the main principle which determines the approach or approaches you use. In other words, depending on the aims of your lesson and your knowledge of your class, one context may favour one approach, while a different context may favour another.

Task 5

Reflecting on your own experience, try to describe how you best learn mathematics.
Some of the following may help you to frame your response:
- by working from textbooks;
- by discussing it with other individuals;
- by working as part of a group (as opposed to merely in a group);
- by working and thinking alone;
- by using concrete resources.

Compare your responses with one or more from other adults and children and note any similarities or differences. Do your school's policy statements offer any advice on this?
At the most simplistic level, there are two ways of teaching mathematics. One is to provide children with a range of experiences so that they may absorb the concepts embedded in them; the other is to provide an example of the concept and give the children lots of further examples to practise it. Each method has its merits, and drawbacks if used exclusively.

 ## How confident are you in your own knowledge of maths?

Even though you may not have been involved in any school-based maths for some time, the above sections should have exposed any 'hidden' aspects of the subject which may have become part of your everyday life.

Task 6

Choose and mark a point in one of the regions in Figure 1.1 which best reflects your current stance and attitude towards maths.
For example, a point in the top left corner would signify a person who is very confident in the subject but does not enjoy it very much. Record why you've chosen to position your point as you have. At the end of the book you will be asked to refer back to this and justify your new position (or why you've not moved) on the diagram.

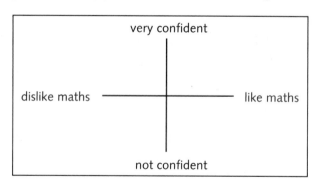

Figure 1.1 Your current attitude to maths

The Government has been concerned for some time about teachers' subject knowledge in mathematics. The requirement for all candidates to have an O Level or GCSE in the subject means that all teachers in schools already have this very basic qualification. Circular 4/98 which was entitled *Teaching: High Status, High Standards* (DfEE 1998) laid down much stronger requirements for trainees to demonstrate their subject knowledge and understanding and their competence in using this knowledge in their teaching. Appendix D of the circular details the Initial Teacher Training Curriculum for Primary Mathematics.

Task 7

Read Section C of Annex D (DfEE 1998) which sets out a body of subject knowledge that is required by all trainees if they are to successfully complete their course.
Tick in pencil all those sections, where you feel confident. Highlight areas on which you will need to work. Be honest! By the end of the course you are expected to know about and understand:

- The real number system;
- Indices;
- Number operations and algebra;
- Equations, functions and graphs;
- Mathematical reasoning and proof;
- Measures;
- Shape and space;
- Probability and statistics.

Responses to subject knowledge initiatives

When Circular 4/98 was published, ITTs (Initial Teacher Training Institutions) looked at various ways in which they could audit and support subject knowledge. This was done in several ways.

1. **Subject Audits** Most developed their own audit system which tested trainees and identified specific areas of need. Some institutions did this prior to candidates being accepted on a course. A candidate, albeit with a GCSE qualification, might not be accepted on the course if he or she failed the initial test. Taught courses were then adapted to ensure that trainees gained the necessary subject knowledge. This has had implications on course content. Trainee teachers spend much more time studying mathematics at their own level, rather than how to teach it to primary school children.

2. **Skills Needs Assessment** As teacher training is moving towards more flexible routes, Skills Needs Assessment Tests have been developed – both by central government agencies such as the TTA (Teacher Training Agency), but also by commercial publishers. These Skills Needs Assessment Tests are more directly related to the contents of Circular 4/98. Some LEAs involved in teacher training as the Recommending Body for the Graduate Teaching Route, allow self-certification of Skills Needs, but most Recommending Bodies (RBs), including ITTs, have a much stronger policy. Self-certification of Skills Needs is very similar to that required in Task 7. The TTA provide a CD-ROM for assessment of needs.

3. **Commercial publishers** Several excellent publications have been produced to support subject knowledge. The TTA acknowledged the use of these publications by asking publishers to bid for a TTA kitemark. The list of 'kitemarked' books is rapidly increasing. A catalogue has been produced and trainees should visit the TTA website for more details. (See 'Useful websites' at the back of this book for the address.) There are also a number of books which address both subject knowledge and teaching mathematics. Several of these make excellent reading, although they lack the TTA kitemark.

4. **Websites** There are now various websites which address the subject, several of which are interactive. As the websites constantly change, only a few are mentioned in the 'Useful websites' section at the back of this book and you should make a search for such sites. The TTA and *TES (Times Educational Supplement)* websites make good starting points. A TTA publication list can be found at: www.canteach.gov.uk

5. **QTS Skills Test** In July 2000, the first government Skills Test in Numeracy was taken by trainees. This was a paper-based test, but by February 2001 this had been converted into a computer test. The TTA publishes a free comprehensive training pack and information booklet for trainees entitled *Assessing your needs in literacy, mathematics, science: Needs assessment materials* (TTA 1999). **All trainees should have a copy of this and make sure that they register for the tests via the Internet.** The TTA have set up an e-mail helpline on their website. The pack materials are also available via the TTA website and on CD-ROM. They include:

- A general introduction;
- Purpose of the tests and to whom they apply;
- How to register for and book a test;
- How to take a test;
- Frequently asked questions on the tests and the computerised system;
- More detail on the content areas for the tests and how these are tested;
- A glossary of technical words used in the tests;
- A list of recommended reading and useful web addresses;
- A feedback form.

The website will also include ten numeracy demonstration questions (completed answers and commentaries on how to reach the answers), and 35 further *numeracy* questions with answers.

A note of caution – it is important that you do not see the mathematics curriculum as just passing the QTS Skills Test. Mathematics is a fascinating subject to teach and there is a wealth of research about what makes for effective teaching and learning. The *TES* provides a good starting point for this and the website for the National Numeracy Strategy (see 'Useful websites' for address) also details research findings about good primary practice.

The Mathematics Curriculum Guide

In this guide we have tried to combine the two elements of best courses available to trainees. There is information and task setting which supports student subject knowledge. There is also information and task setting which supports classroom teaching. You will need to look beyond the subject knowledge element to become a good primary mathematics teacher. One of the guide's authors remembers having an appalling secondary school mathematics teacher, who had taken the subject to a higher degree level.

Two books have proved themselves to be good basic texts for trainee teachers and you are well advised to buy them, as well as at least one of the subject knowledge books listed below.

Haylock, D. (2001)   *Mathematics Explained for Primary Teachers* (2nd edn) London: Paul Chapman Publishing.

Liebeck, P. (1990)   *How Children Learn Mathematics: A Guide for Parents and Teachers.* London: Penguin.

Resources dealing with subject knowledge

Cooke, H. (2001)   *Passport to Professional Numeracy.* London: David Fulton Publishers.

Jennings, S. and Dunne, R. (1997)   *Mathematics for Primary Teachers: An audit and self-study guide.* London: Letts Educational.

Mooney, C. *et al.* (2000)   *Primary Mathematics: Knowledge and Understanding.* Exeter: Learning Matters.

Open University (1998) *M521*   *Passport to Mathematics.* Milton Keynes: OU.

Suggate, J. *et al.* (2001)   *Mathematical Knowledge for Primary Teachers*, 2nd Edn. London: David Fulton Publishers.

TTA (1999)   *Assessing your needs in literacy, mathematics, science: Needs assessment materials* (CD-ROM).

Suggestions for additional subject knowledge titles (including other TTA publications) can be found on the TTA website at www.teach-tta.gov.uk

Chapter 2

The National Curriculum for mathematics

Objectives

After working through this chapter you will:

- have a clear idea of the structure of the National Curriculum for mathematics;
- understand the nature of long-, medium- and short-term planning;
- understand the nature and role of its attainment targets in assessment.

1 Structure

Mathematics is one of the core subjects of the National Curriculum. Its programmes of study (PoS), set out the minimum content to be taught at each key stage. You will need to have your copy of *The National Curriculum 2000* (DfEE/QCA 1999) to hand at all times as reference for this unit.

However, while it is convenient to identify the mathematics content in terms of individual sections you should notice that the programme of study headings for each key stage strongly emphasise how the rich interconnections between them can be exploited in order to integrate children's learning. This approach will help to avoid the fragmentation of children's knowledge, understanding and skills which often leads to a lack of confidence in mathematics.

Task 1

Read through the programmes of study for both key stages. Photocopy the relevant key stage for your course and annotate any areas where your own subject knowledge is challenged. You will need to work on these.

Key Stage 1 trainees should also look at the programme of study for Key Stage 2, and vice versa. Remember many Year 2 children are doing Level 3 work and some children in Key Stage 2 may still be at Key Stage 1 levels. *Curriculum Guidance for the foundation stage* (DfEE 2000b) has a very useful section on mathematical development (See pp. 68–73). This is followed by a section on what children can do and how practitioners can work to develop mathematics in early years settings.

2 Assessment

The Government has established two major assessment tools to gauge children's attainment in mathematics. One is the formal summative statutory test known as the Standard Assessment Test (SAT) held at the end of each key stage and the other is the formative, and usually more informal, continuous teacher assessment (TA) carried out over the entire key stage. The attainment targets and level descriptors can be found at the end of the National Curriculum document.

Task 2

Take one child in your class, or a child known to you. How would you assess the child on each of the attainment targets? Figure 2.1 will help you to record your results for this task.

A.T.	Level	Evidence
Ma 1	Level	
Ma 2	Level	
Ma 3		
Ma 4		

Name of child _____

Figure 2.1 Using formative assessment

Task 3

The National Numeracy Strategy provides a useful overview of short-, medium- and long-term assessment (see pp. 33–37 of the Introduction). Read this and focus a lesson observation schedule on the ways in which the teacher assesses progress.

Chapter 3

The National Numeracy Framework

Objectives

By the end of this chapter you will:

- have reviewed your own understanding of numeracy;
- understand the meaning of numeracy within the terms of the National Framework;
- have an idea of the timetable and mode of implementation;
- be aware of the required structure of lessons within the overall Framework;
- have studied some examples given to assess children's attainment;
- be aware of the location of supportive resources.

1 Numeracy

You may be surprised to learn that 'numeracy' and its associated adjectives, 'numerate' and 'innumerate', have only existed since 1959, compared to 'literate', 'illiterate' and 'illiteracy' which have existed since the early 17th century.

At one time a literate person was someone who was well-read and informed in all the Arts and Humanities, not just in English Literature, but nowadays the meaning appears to be much narrower and is applied generally to those who can read and write. Similarly, the meaning of numeracy (originally applied to those well-versed in the sciences, not just mathematics) has changed over time. Cockcroft (DES 1982) (see paragraphs 35–39) sees numerate persons as having two qualities: an 'at-homeness' with numbers which enables them to cope with the mathematical demands of everyday life, and a facility to appreciate and understand information displayed in a variety of media, such as graphs, charts and tables. For more information see the 'References and further reading' section at the end of this book.

Task 1
Write your definition of numeracy.

Now compare it to the definition given on pp. 3–4 of the Introduction to the NNF:
Numerate pupils should:

- have a sense of the size of a number and where it fits into the number system;
- know by heart number facts such as number bonds, multiplication tables, doubles and halves;

- use what they know by heart to figure out answers mentally;
- calculate accurately and efficiently, both mentally and with pencil and paper, drawing on a range of calculation strategies;
- recognise when it is appropriate to use a calculator and be able to do so effectively;
- make sense of number problems, including non-routine problems, and recognise the operations needed to solve them;
- explain their methods and reasoning, using correct mathematical terms;
- judge whether their answers are reasonable and have strategies for checking them where necessary;
- suggest suitable units for measuring, and make sensible estimates of measurements;
- explain and make predictions from the numbers in graphs, diagrams, charts and tables.

The Framework

To ensure the above desired outcomes are met for as many children as possible, the Framework proposes four principles essential for achieving them:

- mathematics lessons every day;
- direct teaching and interactive oral work with the whole class and groups;
- an emphasis on mental calculation;
- controlled differentiation, with all pupils engaged in mathematics related to a common theme.

Furthermore, the Strategy goes on to detail how a typical 45–60 minute lesson should be structured:

Introduction (5–10 minutes)

Oral work and mental calculation with the whole class; aimed at rehearsing and sharpening skills and carried out at a brisk pace. Typically this will include (depending on the year group):

- counting in steps of different sizes, including chanting and practising instant recall of number facts;
- figuring out new facts from known;
- developing and explaining mental strategies;
- discussing ways of remembering important facts;
- reviewing an activity done at home.

Main teaching activity (30–40 minutes)

Targeting and working with the whole class, groups, pairs or individuals; aimed at introducing a new topic, extending a previous one, developing vocabulary, using and applying concepts and skills. Typically this will include:

- clarifying to the class what they will learn;
- making links with previous learning;
- keeping all children on-task;
- giving deadlines to complete work.

Plenary (10–15 minutes)
Working with the whole class; aimed at maintaining momentum, summarising key ideas and facts, indicating what the next stage in progression will be, crisply closing the lesson, evaluating its outcomes. Typically this will include:

- asking children to present their outcomes to the class for discussion;
- helping them to reflect and remember key findings;
- informally assessing and giving feedback;
- helping children to sort out misconceptions and misunderstandings;
- setting personal targets and tasks to do at home to extend and reinforce school work.

Task 2

If possible watch the NNS video which forms part of the *Three-day course tutor's pack* **(DfEE 1999b) and should be found in all schools. Concentrate on Sequence 3, the complete mathematics lesson with Year 6. This enables you to see how the lesson is structured. Watch the whole lesson first and then return to each section and identify different teaching strategies used.**

The author(s) of the Framework are keen to point out that the three-part structure described above is not a rigid, inflexible recipe to be followed.

- There are many different kinds of lessons which fit the structure
- Teachers should use the opportunities open to them to provide variety
- They should exercise their professional judgement to make sure that the lesson is suitable for the age range of the class, the spread of attainment within the class and what is being taught.

The course notes accompanying the video suggest that:
The structure helps to ensure that teachers:

- Plan lessons that set high expectations of all children
- Focus upon a specific aspect of mathematics
- Increase the amount of time spent on direct teaching to the whole class or group
- Spend more time teaching the whole class.

Task 3

Use the National Numeracy Strategy teaching checklist below, to note aspects of teaching on the video sequence or a lesson seen in a classroom. Remember no single lesson will contain all the features listed.

As an introduction, the teacher:

- Gives a clear start to the lesson
- Maintains a brisk pace
- Provides a variety of short oral and mental activities
- Asks a range of open and closed questions
- Makes sure that all children can see the teacher clearly and take part in the lesson
- Targets individuals, pairs or small groups with particular questions
- Uses children's responses to make an informal assessment
- Makes sure any support staff give discreet help to certain children
- Avoids disruption from too much movement of children around the room
- Avoids running over time and moves smoothly to the next part of the lesson.

In the main activity, the teacher:
- Makes clear to the children what they will learn
- Makes links to previous lessons or to work in other subjects
- Tells children what work they will do and how long it should take
- Tells children what, if anything, they need to prepare for the plenary session
- Maintains pace and gives children a deadline for completing their work.

When working directly with the whole class, the teacher:
- Demonstrates and explains ideas and methods of using a board, flipchart, computer, OHP
- Highlights new vocabulary, notation or terms and gets children to use them in their oral and written work
- Involves children interactively through carefully planned questioning
- Asks children to offer their methods and solutions for discussion
- Ensures that children with particular learning needs in mathematics are supported effectively with appropriate resources, wall displays or adult help
- Identifies and corrects any misunderstandings or forgotten ideas
- Uses mistakes as teaching points.

When working directly with groups, the teacher:
- Has a manageable number of groups (usually a maximum of four)
- Gives a clear introduction to tasks
- Sets clear time scales and expectations for the tasks
- Ensures the degree of differentiation is manageable (for example, by providing linked tasks on the same theme, usually at no more than three levels of difficulty)
- Ensures that children do not have to wait long for their turn
- Maintains all children's interest and motivation and makes sure that they are on-task
- Sits and works intensively with one or two of the groups (does not flit among them)
- Makes appropriate use of any support staff or adult helpers
- Avoids interruption by making sure that those working independently know
  - where to find the resources
  - what to do before asking for help
  - what to do if they finish early.

When working directly with individuals or pairs, the teacher:
- Keeps the children working on related activities, exercises or problems
- Targets individuals or pairs for particular questioning or support
- Encourages children to discuss and cooperate during paired work.

In the plenary, the teacher:
- Makes sure that there is sufficient time for the plenary
- Draws together what has been learned, highlighting key facts, ideas and vocabulary, and what needs to be remembered
- Indicates links with previous work, or where the work is leading
- Brings the lesson to a close, reflecting on what has been achieved.

General management features:
- Seating arrangements allow children to see demonstrations and resources clearly
- Resources and vocabulary have been prepared for use in the lesson
- Any classroom assistants have been fully briefed and are aware of their role.

This checklist and the lesson observation form in Figure 3.1 can also be used to help your own lesson planning and teaching.

Class: Year group:	Little/some/ much evidence	Comments
Teaching High expectations – with children told what they will learn		
Well-structured lesson and suitable pace		
High proportion of direct teaching, making good use of resources		
Oral and mental work		
Effective differentiation and questioning in whole-class work to involve all children		
Mathematical vocabulary developed and used correctly		
Variety of opportunity, children expected to demonstrate and explain, discuss, practise, solve problems, do homework		
Manageable differentiation: differentiation group activities limited to no more than three, all linked to a common theme		
Class/resources organised so teacher can work with group without interruption		
Varied opportunities to watch, listen, be shown, do practical work, practise, discuss, solve problems		
Purposeful plenary: key aspects reinforced; misconceptions dealt with		
Any support staff are deployed well		
Attainment in general: above/about the same as/below the expectations for the age group indicated by the Framework's yearly teaching programme		
Attainment of particular pupil groups e.g. children with Special Educational Needs (SEN), children learning English as an additional language		
Children's attitudes towards learning Listen attentively Participate confidently and speak audibly Persevere and concentrate Are enthusiastic about mathematics Work independently without direct supervision Work well with a partner or in a group Select and use resources sensibly		

Figure 3.1 National Numeracy Framework lesson observation form

Task 4
Observe a numeracy lesson, either on video or in a classroom using the schedule in Figure 3.2.

Weekly planning

The National Numeracy Framework has been adopted very successfully by the vast majority of English schools. Most schools have adapted it to suit the needs of their own pupils and medium- and short-term planning reflect this.

Figure 3.2 is an example of the way in which one school carries out its weekly planning. The teachers write down their planning for Monday to Wednesday. The teacher then looks at children's progress during the first three days and plans for Thursday and Friday are informed by this. Figure 3.3 shows an example of planning using this format. Figure 3.4 shows an example of a PGCE student's weekly planning on her first practice.

Note that all three planning sheets have objectives for the mental starter and main activity. However, the plenary session stands without any objectives. The plenary session can be used for several different purposes and it is useful for student teachers to focus on a key objective for this part of the Numeracy lesson as well. This could be:
- Asking the children to present and explain their work
- Marking work done in the lesson
- Questioning children, assessing work informally and rectifying misconceptions
- Generalising a rule from examples generated by the class
- Reminding children about personal targets and highlighting progress
- Drawing together what has been learned
- Summarising key ideas and vocabulary
- Discussing problems that can now be solved
- Making links to other work
- Discussing briefly what the class will go on to do next
- Setting homework.

Perhaps you can think of some more!

Year_____ Class_____ Week_____

	Key vocabulary	Mental/oral objectives	Main activity objectives			Plenary	Resources
		Activities	Activities	Differentiation			
Mon							
Tues							
Wed						Assessment Plenary	
Thu		Key questions	Formative assessment				
Fri							
		Children not reaching objectives:	Children exceeding objectives:			Notes:	

Figure 3.2 Weekly planning sheet for mathematics

Year 2   Class 2   Week 6

	Key vocabulary	Mental/oral objectives Count on in 5s from and back to zero or any small number. Count in 100s to 1000 from and back to zero.		Main activity objectives Use mathematical vocabulary to describe position, direction, movement. Recognise whole, half and quarter turns to L/R, clockwise, anticlockwise. Know a right angle is a measure of a quarter turn – recognise L shape in ☐ and ☐. Give instructions for route with straight lines and quarter turns.		Plenary	Resources
		Activities		**Activities**	**Differentiation**		
Mon	Fives, hundreds, zero. Full, halves, quarter turns, Right angles, clockwise/ anticlockwise.	Count on in 5s from and back to zero – up to 100. 5 x table		Revise turns. Follow a route – straight lines and quarter turns to L/R. Routes around classroom – children to give instruction.	Give directions – to follow a route – cars on mat – straight lines and quarter L/R turns. Plan a route around classroom. Work in 2 small groups – record on copymaster 20. Support. Straight ahead, L/R quarter turns. Use Nelson enlarged maze.	Revise turns.	Nelson Copymaster 20. Cars, street map, large batteries for robot, maze, pens, extension Nelson books.
Tues	"	"		Right angles – as a measure of quarter turn – L/R. Identify in squares and rectangles. Make L shape by folding paper twice.	L in capital letters. Draw carefully and mark with x.	Right angles. Look at capital letters.	Paper to fold.
Wed	"	5s from small number and back to zero. 5 x table		(Use robot – instructions) Directions around classroom.	Support – work through Nelson routes. Directions activity – Nelson. Nelson routes. Support – Nelson directions activity. Give each other directions around classroom. Cars directions – swap.	**Assessment Plenary**	
	Key questions			**Formative assessment**			
Thu		Number revision					
Fri							
	Children not reaching objectives:			Children exceeding objectives:		Notes:	

Figure 3.3 Completed weekly planning sheet for mathematics

W/B 13th November   Class Year 4M

Key vocabulary

Units; ones; tens; hundreds; digit; calculate; money; coin; note; penny; pound; cost; add on; take away; count; count back; more; less; follow me; double.

Day	Mental maths	Main teaching activity	Plenary	Assessment
Mon	OBJECTIVE: children will be taught to... Read and write whole numbers to at least 10,000 in figures and words. PUT UP THE NUMBER: Hold up the given digits to show the given number (to at least 10,000).	OBJECTIVE: children will be taught to... Use addition and subtraction to solve word problems involving numbers in 'real life' including money, using one or more steps.	Review and discuss strategies used.	Continuous through: Observing the children. Listening and talking with the children. Marking children's work.
Tues	OBJECTIVE: children will be taught to... Add/subtract 1, 10, 100, or 1,000 from any integer up to 10,000. STEPPING STONES: Count on or back in 10s, 100s or 1,000s from any whole number up to 10,000.	MONEY AND 'REAL LIFE' PROBLEMS: Solve money problems written in words. Worksheets: Less able 'Which Coin' sheet 1. More able 'Back to School'. Extension task 'Which Coin 2'. OBJECTIVE: Children will be taught to... Use all four operations to solve word problems involving numbers in 'real life', including money. MONEY AND 'REAL LIFE' PROBLEMS: Solve money problems written in words. Worksheet: At the Greengrocers' (whole class). Less able use 100 square, multiplication square and plastic money. Extension task 'The Fair'.	Work through a few of the children's own money word problems.	
Wed	OBJECTIVE: children will be taught to... Make the amount you give them up to £1. MAKE £1: Using big coins as a stimuli.	OBJECTIVE: Children will be taught to... Use all four operations to solve word problems involving numbers in 'real life', including money. MONEY IN 'REAL LIFE' PROBLEMS: Solve money problems written in words. Worksheet: 'At the Fair' (whole class). Less able use 100 square, multiplication square and plastic money. Extension task 'School Visit'.	Work through a few of the children's own money word problems.	Continuous through: Observing the children. Listening and talking with the children. Marking children's work.
Thu	OBJECTIVE: children will be taught to... Derive quickly, double of all whole numbers up to 50. FOLLOW ME GAME: Basic doubles of whole numbers to 50.	OBJECTIVE: Children will be taught to... Check the sum of several numbers by adding in reverse order. MAKING DECISIONS/CHECKING RESULTS: Less able use 100 square, multiplication square. Whole class to answer questions written on the board.	Work through a few questions on the board. Check answers with an equivalent calculation.	Continuous through: Observing the children. Listening and talking with the children. Marking children's work.
Fri	OBJECTIVE: children will be taught to... Know by heart multiplication facts for 2, 3, 4, and 5, times-tables. FOLLOW ME GAME: Recall multiplication facts X2, X3, X4, X5.	OBJECTIVE: Children will be taught to... Choose and use appropriate number operations and appropriate ways of calculating to solve problems. MAKING DECISIONS/CHECKING RESULTS: Which operation? Prepared worksheet 'You Choose'.	Go through questions and discuss methods and strategies as well as answers. Choose a few children to demonstrate how they checked they had the correct answer.	Continuous through: Observing the children. Listening and talking with the children. Marking children's work.

Figure 3.4 Numeracy planner

Lesson Planning

Trainee teachers do not begin with the medium- and weekly-term planning for their teaching. Initially they will start with planning for a short part of the numeracy lesson. Often this is the mental starter, but may be some small group work. Eventually, they will start to plan for the whole of the lesson and the template in Figure 3.5 provides a starting point. After the template there are some additional guidance notes.

Class _____ Set (if appropriate) _____ Date _____
Length of sessions _____
Number of children _____ Age of children _____

Oral/mental starter
- Objectives
- Key vocabulary
- Interactive teaching activities.

Main teaching activity
- Objectives
- Introduction (where appropriate)
- Activities (including details of differentiation)
- Key questions
- Organisation, including your teaching role(s).

Plenary
- Focus/objectives
- Activity/ies
- Opportunities for homework (where appropriate).

Resources

Assessment (where appropriate):
- What is being assessed?
- How is this being assessed?
- How will you know whether this has been achieved?

Briefing notes for support workers (if applicable).

Figure 3.5 Template for a mathematics lesson plan

Task 5

Plan a numeracy lesson or part of a numeracy lesson using this format.
Include the lesson and its evaluation in your file.

These notes will help you to plan effective lessons

- *Identify clearly the learning objectives.* These should be more specific versions of the objectives from the Yearly Teaching Programmes contained in the NNF. They should be specific, for example sizes of numbers and particular types of measures. Words and phrases from the outcomes in the supplements of examples will help. Normally you should identify one, or at most two objectives.
- *Specify what vocabulary will be explicitly addressed,* and whether this is consolidation or whether it is a new piece of vocabulary.
- *State what resources you will use.* This should include important mathematical resources as well as things like pencil and paper.

- *Describe any assessment activities.* These may not occur in every session, but you may decide to use, for example, a plenary, or an Oral and mental starter to find out informally how much the children have understood.

The following instructions clarify the different structures that you should follow within each of the three parts.

- *For the Oral and mental starter (about 5–10 minutes)*
  Clarify the focus of this part of the lesson, and what aspects of mental calculation you are concentrating on. Indicate the classroom organisation. Make a list of the activities you will pursue in order. Write down questions, and the strategies you will be expecting to teach, or children to adopt. Give some indication of how you intend to address the different abilities within the class. Give an appropriate timing.

- *For the Main teaching activity (about 30–40 minutes)*
  If you are giving an 'introduction', write this out clearly, specifying what you are teaching and how you will do this, giving the examples you intend to use, and the questions you will ask. For the children's working session, you should clarify how this will be organised, whether group, pairs, individuals, etc. and how long the children are expected to take on the activities. You should also indicate the sizes of the groups and their abilities in relation to the topic (i.e. how the differentiation is occurring). Give examples of worksheets or pages from books which relate to these differentiated objectives. You should have no more than three different groups. You should also record precisely what you will do during the lesson. Give an indication of timing, with a breakdown of the different parts of the session.

- *For the Plenary session (about 10–15 minutes)*
  Clarify the type of activities that will be carried out during this part of the lesson, and their purpose. Write down key ideas which you intend to stress. Indicate the organisation and timing. If homework is being given, specify what this is.

After the lesson you will need to carry out an Evaluation. This should review the whole lesson, and your part in it, examining the appropriateness of your planning, including your preparedness, your organisation, your performance, your responses to the children's questions or difficulties and the children's response to the lesson and to you.

Assessment

You need to clarify how you intend to assess the children. One way in which this can be done is to:

1. State your points for assessment by choosing six main objectives against which you intend to assess the children. These objectives may need to be refined to be made as explicit as possible.

2. Against each of these, state your proposed method of assessment and say how you will know if the child has demonstrated understanding.

You will record the results of your assessments by making notes about each child. This should include the child's responses to your particular assessment activities and your conclusions about his or her mathematical understanding. When assessment is set out clearly as shown in Figure 3.6, it becomes possible for a trained support worker to undertake the assessment while working with small groups of children.

This method of assessment is ideal when you are only responsible for small groups. It enables you to focus your planning and also identify different ways in which children learn mathematics. It also identifies common misconceptions and enables you to prepare for these in your future planning.

Points for assessment	Method of assessment	How will I know if the child has demonstrated understanding?
From the Framework: Point 1: 'Read and write whole numbers to at least 100 in figures and words.' Specifically, I intend to 'examine the children's abilities to read whole numbers to 100 in figures'.	Play a 'bingo-style' game with a group of four children. The children each have a board, with random numbers between 20 and 100. Each child takes it in turn to be the 'caller'. The caller turns over the top card from a pack of number cards (20 to 100 in random order). The caller reads out the number and any child with that number on their board is able to cover it.	When 'calling' out the numbers the child is able, without prompts, to correctly read the numbers. The child is able to recognise the numbers when they are called out and hence cover these on the boards. In order to judge that a child is able to read whole numbers to 100, I would not expect more than one minor error by the child, and for the child to be able to self-correct.

Figure 3.6 Recording assessment results

Assessment within the Numeracy Framework

The NNF has an extremely helpful section on assessment. Many of the statements made are applicable in other subject areas and there is a real attempt to try and make assessment manageable. The Assessment section in the document (pp. 33–37 of the Introduction) covers:

- Short-term assessments
- Medium-term assessments, including individual targets for pupils and keeping parents informed
- Long-term assessments
- Passing on information about pupils' attainment and progress.

The Teaching programme in the planning framework itself is supplemented by examples, targets and links to the Teaching programme for each school year. These also help to make assessment much more precise. Like the Teaching programme, these supplements of examples cover:

- Numbers and the number system
- Calculations
- Solving problems
- Handling data (Key Stage 2 only)
- Measures
- Shape and space.

There is also a supplement of examples for reception classes, which covers:
- Counting and recognising numbers
- Adding and subtracting
- Solving problems
- Measures
- Shape and Space.

Of course the Numeracy Strategy was published some time before the foundation stage materials were sent into schools. This raised challenges in relation to planning for the foundation stage in reception classes, where the *Curriculum Guidance for the foundation stage* (QCA/DfEE 2000) makes no mention of the National Numeracy Strategy in its section on mathematical development. The section in this document covers *Number* and *Shape, space and measures*. There is also a much greater emphasis on children's mathematical development arising out of daily experiences in a rich and interesting environment.

Role of additional adults in the classroom

The support materials provided for Numeracy Coordinators emphasised that additional adults had an important role in helping teachers to meet the needs of particular children. Student teachers need to see that their planning should involve these additional workers. Usually they will find that the school has already:
- Got a programme of briefing adults on lesson objectives, mathematical vocabulary and key questions to ask;
- Made sure that the additional adults working in the classroom are well prepared and know which children to support.

General guidance given to Numeracy Coordinators suggests that:
1. **In whole-class sessions**, additional adults can:
   - Be strategically positioned near particular individuals or groups to support and encourage responses, e.g. from shy and reticent children;
   - Support a child with visual impairment by using a hand-held whiteboard to reproduce what is on the main board;
   - Sign or translate core vocabulary or phrases;
   - Keep children on-task;
   - Help children to use specific individual resources e.g. personal number cards, table top number lines, or individualised ICT resources linked to the child's Individual Education Plan (IEP).
2. **In group work,** additional adults can:
   - Support individual children or groups;
   - Keep children focused and on-task;
   - Help maintain pace;
   - Remind children of teaching points and help them interpret instructions correctly;
   - Question children and prompt responses, based on suggestions from the teacher;
   - Emphasise correct use of mathematical vocabulary;
   - Explain extension tasks.
3. For the **plenary**, additional adults can:
   - Prepare children to feed back on the work they have been doing;
   - Prompt children as they go along and help them explain their strategies;
   - Monitor the responses of particular children.

Mathematical vocabulary

The Framework for the NNS places great importance on the use of correct terminology. For this reason the DfEE (1999c) published a special 32-page booklet entitled *National Numeracy Strategy Mathematical Vocabulary*, which was included in the materials sent into schools by the DfEE. This was seen as essential because children's failure to understand mathematical vocabulary shows itself in three main ways – they do not respond to questions in lessons; they cannot do a task they are set and/or they do poorly in tests.

The book provides four pages of vocabulary checklists for each year group. The first three pages for each year cover mathematical vocabulary relating to the Framework, organised according to its five strands:
- Numbers and the number system
- Calculations
- Solving problems
- Handling data
- Measures, shape and space.

Using and applying mathematics is integrated throughout
The vocabulary book also includes a section on the skill of questioning. It identifies six different types of question such as recalling facts; applying facts; hypothesising or predicting; designing and comparing procedures; interpreting results and applying reasoning. This is followed by two pages of open and closed questions to help teachers – and trainees – to promote good dialogue and interaction in mathematics lessons. There are many useful lessons here for other areas of the curriculum.

Homework
As well as the mathematics vocabulary book, schools were sent materials to support numeracy in the home. A booklet entitled *At home with numeracy* provides information about strategies for involving parents, a supportive school environment, targets for children, homework and key recommendations and ideas. In a separate booklet called *Sample homework activities*, there are several homework activities given as examples. Many publishers have produced homework schemes to give support to both teachers and parents, for example, the *Maths homework series* (Fleet and Fleet 1997) published by Belair Publications. The NNF makes it quite clear (see pp. 15 and 16) that not all out-of-class work needs to be written work. Some dos and don'ts on homework provided in the Framework include:

- *Do* meet with parents to explain the homework.
- *Do* set some tasks or activities that draw upon the context of the home.
- *Do* provide a means for parents to feedback information about how their child is getting on.
- *Don't* punish children who do not complete their homework.
- *Don't* give homework that requires parents to teach their child some maths.
- *Do* make the homework enjoyable.
- *Do* give children feedback on the homework that they do.
- *Do* encourage governors to visit classrooms and talk to children about their homework.

Governors
All schools should have a Numeracy Governor. As with special educational needs and literacy, there is a nominated governor who takes a special interest in the National Numeracy Strategy and helps to ensure that numeracy issues remain high on the school's agenda. A special booklet entitled *Information for governors* sets out the role of the Numeracy Governor.

Task 6
Re-read the Introduction to the NNF, focusing on the School and class organisation section, which covers areas such as SEN, EAL (English as an Additional Language) and very able pupils.

Chapter 4

Ma2: Number and algebra

Objectives

By the end of this chapter you will:

- understand principles of how children learn to count;
- recognise contexts where children can practise counting;
- appreciate some different modes of counting;
- understand ideas of equivalence and transforming and how these can facilitate children's competence in computation;
- recognise the importance of language in developing knowledge, skills and understanding;
- understand principles of how children learn to add, subtract, multiply and divide whole numbers;
- know how to use underlying principles to extend these ideas to other kinds of numbers;
- understand the principles behind standard algorithms and give reasons for and against their use;
- recognise the importance of developing *ad hoc*, especially mental, methods of computation;
- understand the importance of place value in the structure of our number system;
- be aware of some common errors and misconceptions that children make in number.

Section 1 Learning to count

Task 1
Count the number of squares in Figure 4.1. While you are doing this, focus on your actions and describe how you did it. Compare your method with other adults and children of different ages.

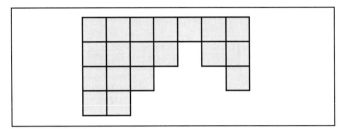

Figure 4.1 Counting the squares

The arrows in Figure 4.2 show some of the different ways that people may count the 19 squares – horizontally, vertically, singly or in clusters. In fact, it would be good practice to check your result by using an alternative approach.

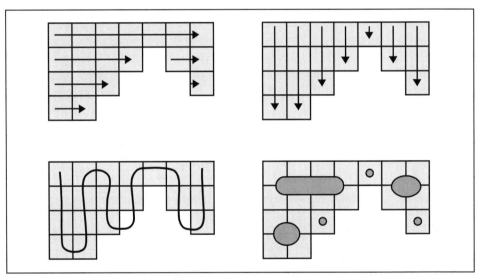

Figure 4.2 Different methods of counting (ATM 1985)

This activity serves to raise your awareness of an important point for both planning your lessons and assessing children's attainment: **that children may reach ostensibly correct conclusions via different but valid (and sometimes invalid) pathways**. Some methods may be more efficient than others and some you may never even have thought of yourself, but these can now be added to your own knowledge. Some methods may be faulty and work only for specific cases, thus it is important to ask children to articulate and share their methods. Having their own methods valued can instil confidence by giving children a sense of ownership and control over their maths.

It is worth now considering just what is involved in the apparently mundane, but in fact surprisingly sophisticated, skill of counting. To help you get a sense of what counting might feel like to young children have a go at the following task.

Task 2

Starting from seven, count up in seventeens until you pass 100. Starting from 104, count down in thirteens.

It would be surprising if you did not find at least part of this task challenging. It is therefore worth reflecting on the mental and physical processes that you used to carry it out. The point being made here is that the task of counting can be made as easy or as difficult as required to cater for a range of children. You might, for example, ask **higher-attaining** children to count up and down in decimal fractions such as 0.3.

You should notice too that varying the starting points forces a range of strategies to come into play. How did you perform the two counts above?

Task 3

Read through pp. 74–77 of the *Curriculum guidance for the foundation stage (QCA/ DfEE 2000).* **Make a note of anything which surprised you.**

Young children, of course, do not enter school with their minds a blank slate, and many between the ages of four and five will already have a partial grasp of these ideas. Depending on a variety of factors some may be able to:

- say the various number names, though not necessarily in the correct order;
- recognise familiar visual number patterns such as those on dice;
- determine visually which is the larger or smaller of two sets of objects;
- be familiar with or recognise 'big' numbers, such as a parent's age or their own house number.

In contrast, some children may not yet link written or printed number symbols with the cardinal value of a set (see below) nor be able to order numbers in the counting sequence according to their cardinal value.

However, by the end of Year 1 the majority of children will be able to count confidently to 10, and beyond. This ability to count is not acquired spontaneously. Children will need to experience a range of activities to help them make their own connections between the conventional sounds of the number names which they recite and the size of a collection of objects. In short, to be considered 'counters' children need to demonstrate that they can:

- say the number names in the right order (the stable order principle);
- match each number name to one, and only one, object (the one-to-one principle);
- count each object in a collection once only;
- recognise that the final number name said is the size or value (numerosity) of the set (the ordinal to cardinal rule);
- know that the order in which objects are counted does not matter (the order is an irrelevant principle);
- know that the cardinal value of a set remains constant even when its objects have been rearranged (conservation of number).

Awareness of the above factors will help you to determine children's current understanding and thus plan and implement activities according to how you perceive their needs.

Another very important general point that should be made here is that, as far as possible, children should see that there is a purpose to their maths, in this case the counting (including the enjoyment of social singing and chanting). As a teacher you need to be aware of, and capitalise on, informal opportunities for this throughout the school day – not just in maths lessons.

Task 4

List the contexts both inside and outside school where children can practise their counting in a relevant context. Examples might include:

- discussing ages, birthdays and birthday cards, badges and candles;
- counting down the days to significant events such as Christmas, using the calendar, talking about the time of day;
- counting the number of children in the class, the numbers of children absent or present, the number having lunches, wearing black shoes, having blue eyes, and so on;
- reading and discussing stories and rhymes where the number of characters or objects increases or decreases.

The National Numeracy Framework will give you plenty of other examples in the 'Supplement of examples: Reception' (section 4).

Section 2   Learning to add and subtract

> The importance of counting as a precursor to making progress in addition and subtraction was probably evident to you in the counting task which you carried out in Section 1 (though you probably used arithmetic to help you to complete the count rather than the other way around!). Not only is counting itself important but, as we shall see below, the way that children count can be a major influence on whether they develop confidence in their mathematics, and number skills in particular.

As an aid to discussion and identifying children's attainment it is useful to list a hierarchy of broad counting strategies for addition, starting from:

- 'count-all', which involves counting each set separately, combining their elements, then counting the aggregated set;
- next comes 'count-on from first', where children count on the number of elements in the second set having started from the first number given;
- this is followed by the more efficient 'count-on from largest', starting from the larger set first and counting on the smaller number of elements in the other set.

These lead on to the higher order strategies of knowing a fact, then deriving new facts from known facts.

Similarly for subtraction the hierarchy begins with:

- 'taking away', count the big set, count the subset being removed, then count the remaining set;
- 'count-back', start from the larger number and count back down the number sequence to find the number remaining;
- 'count-up', start from the number to be subtracted and count up to the number given.

Again, you find that 'simple' addition and subtraction may not be all that simple! The transfer of concrete, physical activity into written, symbolic form (and back again) can be problematic for some children. Similarly, you will now be aware that different models of addition and subtraction exist, even though they may well be represented symbolically in the same way.

A well-known example of children just adding given numbers instead of trying to make sense of a problem is seen in spoof questions, such as: 'A ship is carrying 16 goats and 25 sheep. How old is the captain?' Invariably the answer 41 is given. You might like to try this.

Outcomes like this clearly indicate, as the National Numeracy Strategy is striving to do, that you need to ensure that your pupils are empowered by being able to bring a range of strategies to bear on a particular problem and choose the most appropriate for them.

Task 1

Ask a child to make up a story embodying one of these calculations:

5 + 6   3 + 19   27 + 28   7 – 3   23 – 9

Can you identify which models of counting they could be using?

How might you begin to help a child who seems to have little or no understanding?

Paradoxically, those who fail at number may be doing a more difficult kind of maths than those who succeed. Successful children learn how to derive new facts from old in a flexible way by using equivalences.

The idea of equivalence is one of the 'big ideas' permeating the whole of maths, not just number. Because of this we can 'transform' one operation to another equivalent, but more convenient, form. For instance 17 – 8 might be given immediately as 9, and seem like a known fact, yet it may have been derived instantaneously from knowing that 17 can be decomposed to 9 + 8 (or some other convenient equivalent form) and the 8 removed to leave 9.

Task 2

For each of the following, write down five equivalent calculations, e.g. 39 + 99 = 38 + 100 and so on. Note the strategies you used.

(i)   99 + 43

(ii) 98 – 31

(iii) 6 x 88

(iv) 37 ÷ 4

To maintain equivalence you may have used:

- adding to one number and subtracting the same number from the other in (i);

- adding or subtracting the same number from both in (ii);

- doubling one and halving the other in (iii);

- doubling or halving both numbers in (iv).

The role of language

You have already seen in Chapter 2 how important mathematics vocabulary is. The importance of the role of language in counting is highlighted in a study by Fuson and Kwon (1991) in which they compared the structure of the counting words in a variety of European and Asian languages. English and Chinese counting words, for example, are equivalent in the first decade, one through to ten. However, the next decade shows important differences. What influence do you think this could have on children's ability to count?

English	Chinese
eleven	ten one
twelve	ten two
thirteen	ten three
fourteen	ten four
fifteen	ten five
sixteen	ten six
seventeen	ten seven
eighteen	ten eight
nineteen	ten nine
twenty	two ten
twenty one	two ten one
twenty two	two ten two
. . .	. . .

thirty	three ten
. . .	. . .
one hundred	one hundred
one hundred and one	one hundred one
. . .	. . .
one hundred and twenty five	one hundred two ten five
. . .	. . .
five thousand two hundred and forty one	five thousand two hundred four ten one.

Fuson and Kwon point out further features of the English counting system which make the load on the memory greater and hence make the learning more difficult, compared with the efficient pattern of re-using the first nine numbers as in the Chinese naming system:

- the words 'eleven' and 'twelve' do not indicate their 'ten one' and 'ten two' composition;
- similarly, the irregular pronunciation of 'three' and 'five' in 'thirteen' and 'fifteen' respectively hides the re-use of 'three, four, … eight, nine' with 'teen', to make the 'ten three' to 'ten nine' words;
- in the teen words the 'four' in 'fourteen', for example, is said first, in contrast to all the other decades where it is said second ('twenty four'), again hiding the 'tens-units' structure. (This may be why some children reverse the digits when writing, for example 41 for 14);
- the irregular pronunciation of the decade words 'twenty', 'thirty' and 'fifty' hides the use of 'teen' and 'ty' as modifications of 'ten'.

The structure of the Chinese naming system may help Chinese-speaking children to add and subtract more easily than English speakers: 'eight plus five' is thought of as 'eight plus two from the five, is ten, plus the three left over from the five is 'ten three'. In the English system the 'ten plus three is thirteen' is an extra step which has to be learned rather than being given by the counting sequence 'ten three'. Some useful equivalences arise automatically in Chinese.

Finally, it is worth checking your school's approach to the symbol for zero. In some it is introduced after the number '5' while other schools prefer to leave it until later.

All the above should help you to appreciate that if children can see underlying structures and unifying ideas in their mathematics rather than a large set of fragmented and isolated concepts (relational versus instrumental understanding, Skemp (1979)) they can begin to mentally construct their own rich conceptual structures. (See Cockcroft, DES 1982, paragraph 241.)

Section 3   Using algorithms

It is now time to consider the standard written methods or processes (algorithms) which are most often taught in schools.

Task 1
Set out and perform the calculations below; write down what you actually say aloud or mentally (your script!). Now explain how your methods work for each one:

357 + 408   603 – 247

Did you use words like 'carry', 'borrow', 'pay back', 'go next door'? Can you explain what these terms mean? Compare your method with the one(s) used in your school.

The most commonly-taught written algorithm for subtraction is the so-called 'decomposition' method. However, there is evidence to suggest that outside (and even inside!) school many people do not use standard methods, preferring 'adhocorithms', or 'back of envelope' calculations (idiosyncratic methods which have been somehow gleaned without formal instruction). One of the aims of the NNS is to increase children's computational skills by moving away from the exclusivity of written standard algorithms towards mental methods based on equivalences.

Plunkett (1977) identifies written standard algorithms as being:
- written, and hence permanent and correctable;
- standardised, so it is possible that everyone does the same thing;
- concise, in the sense of summarising the laws of arithmetic used (distributivity and associativity);
- efficient, it's less efficient to add the tens first because of the possible need to subsequently amend their total after the units have been added;
- automatic, in that they can be taught to and carried out by someone who has no understanding of what is happening;
- symbolic, the calculation is done entirely by symbolic manipulation, with no reference to the real world;
- general, they will work for any numbers, big, small or decimal;
- analytic, they require numbers to be broken up into tens and units digits which should be dealt with separately;
- not easily internalised, they don't correspond to the ways that people tend to think about numbers;
- encouraging passivity, people just do them without thinking much about alternatives.

The following examples make clear that children may have only instrumental understanding:

$$
\begin{array}{cccc}
46 & 45 & 24 & \\
\underline{27+} & \underline{-38} & \underline{\times 3} & 2\underline{)3\ 1\ 8} \\
91 & 1 & 612 & 1\quad 9 \\
3 & & &
\end{array}
$$

Paradoxically children who make mistakes like these may be able to perform the calculations accurately using mental methods. So is it the algorithm or the mathematics that they don't understand?

Task 2
Here are some more examples of children's errors when performing addition using 'vertical' algorithms. For each one identify the error(s) and suggest what you might do towards remedying the misunderstanding.

$$
\begin{array}{ccccc}
7 & 15 & 26 & 56 & 123 \\
\underline{12} & \underline{19} & \underline{7} & \underline{28} & 52 \\
82 & 61 & 213 & 74 & \underline{4} \\
 & & & & 219
\end{array}
$$

Your analysis needs to go beyond the obvious 'they've not lined up the columns correctly' as this is focusing solely on the mechanism of the algorithm. There appears to be some fundamental confusion about place value (see Section 4) and you will need to explore this by listening to any children who have similar problems explaining their reasoning. Another aim of the NNS is to make children aware that there are many legitimate, and often mental, alternative ways of performing simple calculations. The written, vertical algorithms are only one of these.

Compare your list with Plunkett's (1977). He identified the attributes of adhocorithms as:
- fleeting, often difficult to catch hold of;
- variable, a class of children may use many different methods;
- flexible, they can be adapted to suit the numbers involved;
- active, in that the user makes a choice and feels in control;
- holistic, working with complete numbers rather than separated tens and units digits – 4 x 35 = 2 x 70 = 140;
- constructive, working from one part of the question towards the answer – 37 + 28: 37, 47, 57, 67, 65;
- not designed for recording (but can be when required), tending to sprawl when written;
- requiring understanding all along;
- iconic, they relate to mental images, such as the number line, or depend on serial enunciation as in 32 + 21: 32, 42, 52, 53;
- able to give an early approximation, because the leftmost digit is calculated first – 145 + 37: 175, 182;
- limited, as they can't be applied to the most difficult calculations – 269 x 23.

Section 4   Place value

Children are given a wide variety of 'concrete' and 'structured' materials to model written calculations.

Task 1
List the most commonly-used resources in your classroom or school. Find out and describe how they are used.

It is possible to be overcome by the wealth of resources, both commercial and home-made, available to help children make the transfer from operating on concrete objects to operating on the symbols that represent them. The most common is probably the Dienes' apparatus to model the decomposition ('exchange' is a more appropriate term) algorithm for subtraction. The apparatus is rarely used as Dienes intended. His ideas are founded on the generic principles of grouping and exchange. His apparatus is often applied specifically and solely to our base ten place value system in demonstrating how the decomposition algorithm, for example, works. Without careful monitoring and discussion it is possible for children to merely manipulate the apparatus without making the mental link with the written representation of the operations being performed.

The reason that our number system is based on groups of ten is probably because we have ten fingers. Have you ever thought about what our system would look like if we had fewer or even more than ten fingers? Surprisingly it would probably look much the same, as the underlying principles would still apply. If, for example, we had only two fingers then our system would resemble that of the binary (2–) digit code used in recording and

TV transmission. If we had sixteen, then it would resemble the hexadecimal (16–) digit code used in some computers. The only major difference would be that in our base 10 (or decimal) system we use only the digits 0 to 9 to represent any number, while in binary arithmetic only 0 and 1 are necessary and in hexadecimal we have to include further symbols to represent numbers up to 15. (These are usually A, B, C, D, E and F to represent 10, 11, 12, 13, 14, and 15 respectively.)

Thus, 'our' 33 in base 10 would be written as 100001 in base 2 and 21 in base 16. This can be off-putting initially but further investigation should reveal the logic behind the systems. It helps to number the values of the columns rather than using letters:

Base 10	**100 10 1**	Base 2	**32 16 8 4 2 1**	Base 16	**16 1**
	3 3		1 00001		2 1

In the base 10 system you will know that 33 represents three tens plus three ones. In binary, 33 is seen as a thirty-two plus one unit, while in hexadecimal it is represented as two sixteens plus one unit. Notice that, just as in base 10, each column has a value of the base times as many as the column to its right.

Just as you might feel uncomfortable operating in the sixteens required by hexadecimal, so children need to abstract the idea of exchange from numbers suited to their current level of development. Hence Dienes' apparatus ranges from materials in base 2 to base 10 and beyond. In base 10, units are represented by small cubes, ten of which can be exchanged for a stick of ten, hundreds by squares of ten sticks and thousands by cubes of ten squares. However, early work involved naming the groupings, ones/units, 'longs', 'flats' and 'blocks', respectively. As a further aid to abstracting the idea of exchange, Dienes also includes triangular and trapezium-shaped pieces (though in practice these seem to be little used) to emphasise that even though shape is varied the mathematical structure is preserved.

Task 2
Write down an example of how you have used a specfic piece of apparatus to help children develop understanding of place value. Now confer with someone else in your own key stage. Then discuss with someone working in another key stage.

Section 5   Multiplication and division

 Multiplication

Task 1
Perform a written calculation for 26 x 34. Note any kind of internal or external 'script' that you use while doing it. Then read through the NNF exemplar for years 1, 2 and 3 (pp. 46 and 47) in section 5 and for years 4, 5 and 6 (pp. 52 and 53) in Section 6. Draft a hierarchical list of activities embodying the multiplication principles gained from your reading.

Compare your algorithm for 26 x 34 with this:

```
      26
    x 34
     780  ←  26 x 30
     104  ←  26 x 4
     884  ←  26 x 34 (780 + 104)
```

Note the differences between this and yours, if any, including how you set it out. Did this method match yours exactly? Were you surprised that it began with the tens digit (in this case the 3)? Would you rather have put the larger number (in this case 34) 'on the top'? Is this method the 'correct' one, or at least better than yours? And were you aware that the algorithm masks, but makes use of, the distributive law?

The commutative law for multiplication means that it is immaterial whether 26 is multiplied by 34 or the other way around, it simply depends on what is more convenient. (Did you check your result by multiplying in a different order?) The important thing is that children are aware that they have a choice. Multiplying by the units or tens digit first is also a matter of choosing, though it could be argued that multiplying by the tens digit initially gives a better first approximation to the answer which may be all that is needed in some situations.

The NNS promotes the use of a range of strategies for multiplication. You have already encountered the use of the strategy of 'doubling' to help derive facts in early addition. This is the multiplication method of the ancient Egyptians and can be placed in context when studying this period of history. It is essentially the same approach as that described converting decimal to binary notation.

Again, for 26 x 34:

1 x 34 = 34
2 x 34 = 68
4 x 34 = 136
8 x 34 = 272
16 x 34 = 544, etc.

Now 26 = 16 + 8 + 2   so 26 x 34 = (16 x 34) + (8 x 34)+ (2 x 34) which (from the calculation above) gives 544 + 272 + 68 = 884.

Notice that this again makes use of the distributive law. Its major advantage is that the mathematics of the method is transparent and requires no knowledge of multiplication tables, as does the standard algorithm. Everything can be carried out by addition.

Another algorithm is called the 'gelosia method' (believed to be named after the latticed windows or *gelosia* of Venetian buildings).

Again, using the same problem, the results of the individual multiplications 3 x 6, 3 x 2, 4 x 6, 4 x 2 are placed in the triangular lattices as shown in Figure 4.3 and added diagonally in the direction of the arrows starting from the bottom right triangle. Any tens are added to the next window on the left. The results are placed underneath the squares as shown and the answer read from left to right. (This is much easier to understand when it is demonstrated, rather than written!)

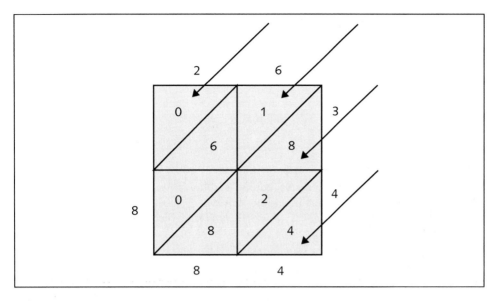

Figure 4.3 The gelosia method of multiplication

Task 2

Try this yourself on 326 x 54. You will need to use a 3 x 2 grid split into triangles as in Figure 4.3.

You may also come across this method in the form of rods of numbers called 'Napier's bones'. These are named after John Napier (1617) the inventor of logarithms.

These methods are offered as alternatives to promote interest and raise questions in children about how they work. But there is a moral point here too – do we teach children such 'tricks' or should, and can, everything be taught for complete understanding?

 Division

Task 3

Read the relevant sections on division in the NNF for years 1–3 and 4–6 (Sections 5 and 6).

Of all the standard algorithms, the one used for long division is probably the most opaque. The use of the repeated subtraction model for short division is well worth pursuing for long division, as the underlying structure is the same and therefore helps to reduce the memory load. *Ad hoc* methods, especially those of rounding and estimating results, are probably more important, especially in checking that calculator results are an appropriate size.

It is worth noting here that, just as triples of numbers such as 3, 4 and 7 are linked by addition and subtraction (if two are known then this defines the other), this also applies to triples connected by multiplication and division. So for 3, 4 and 12, if two are known then the third is defined automatically. For example:

$$3 + 4 = 7 \qquad\qquad 3 \times 4 = 12$$
$$7 - 3 = 4 \qquad \text{and} \qquad 3 = 12 \div 4$$
$$7 - 4 = 3 \qquad\qquad 4 = 12 \div 3$$

There is a strong case for learning tables, just as there is a case for learning number bonds, but mere chanting must be supplemented with other activities. Fielker (*TES* 1996) points out that the tables are a sophisticated organisation of 121 number facts and asks the question: 'In what other situation do we ask children to start to learn the organisation before they have anything to organise?' He follows this with an anecdote about a boy who asked his father to test him because he knew his seven-times table. The father said: 'OK. What's 56?' He was told that this wasn't fair!

Task 4

What activities if any are used in your school for 'learning tables'? Compare what happens in your school with what happens in another school.

Now read the relevant sections of the NNF on rapid recall of multiplication and division facts.

Section 6 Extending the number system

So far we have focused on what are known as the counting numbers – the positive whole numbers 1, 2, 3, and so on, and zero. The results of operations such as 5 – 8, and 3 ÷ 4, however, force us to extend our number system to include 'directed numbers' and fractions.

 Number lines

Number lines are a very useful device for representing and operating on numbers holistically. Every child should have a number line available for personal use, as well as a classroom model for group or class activities. According to the child's developmental stage these might range from 0–10, graduated in units, to 0–100, graduated in decimal fractions (a measuring tape is a practical, everyday example of a number line!). The ultimate aim is for children to make use of the 'empty' number line – for them to sketch a line and mark in graduations appropriate to the context in which they are working as shown in Figure 4.4. For example:

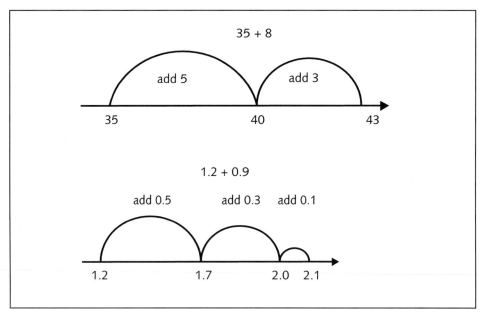

Figure 4.4 Using number lines

Directed numbers

Task 1

Perform these calculations, noting whatever script you use to work them out.

$$
\begin{array}{ll}
6 - 9 & -6 + -9 \\
6 \ - \ -9 & -9 - 6 \\
-9 \ - \ -6 &
\end{array}
$$

Apart from fractions, no other area of mathematics is taught and learned in such an instrumental way, being especially hindered by inappropriate generalisations, rules and language.

Fractions

In spite of predictions of the demise of fractions with the arrival of decimalisation, understanding fractions, and the operations upon them, continues to be a source of concern for many children and adults, including teachers.

Before planning any lesson it is useful to be aware of potential misconceptions and errors that children commonly make. This is particularly true for fractions.

Task 2

Jot down some ideas about why fractions might be difficult to learn.
Compare your response with these:
- a view of fractions that is limited to a part-whole model (see below);
- the existence of some inappropriate models of fractions;
- a reluctance to accept that fractions are numbers;
- a dependence on algorithms that have been learned by rote;
- confusing terminology such as 'share by' and 'divide into';
- a failure to realise that properties true for counting numbers are not necessarily true for fractions;
- the emphasis on partial truths at earlier stages which are no longer true for fractions such as 'multiplying makes bigger'.

Task 3

Jot down as many words and phrases as possible that you associate with 'fractions'. Now write explanations of what they mean to you.
You may have listed words and phrases such as: 'of means multiply'; 'cancel down'; 'share by'; 'divide into'; 'top heavy'; 'numerator and denominator'; 'mixed number'; 'equivalent fraction'; 'do the same to the bottom as the top'; and so on. Did you manage to explain what they meant to your own satisfaction? For example, you may be able to perform a division of one fraction by another using the 'turn upside down and multiply' rule, but can you explain why it works?

Children's early experience of fractions in maths lessons usually consists of cutting up and/or reassembling a small number of size-equivalent pieces of some 'whole' shapes, usually squares or circles of different proportions. This should be accompanied by appropriate vocabulary and language before formally introducing the symbols for half, quarter and so on. However, care should be taken since there is potential for confusion here.

Task 4

Shade in half of each of the shapes in Figure 4.5. How many different ways can you do this for each one?

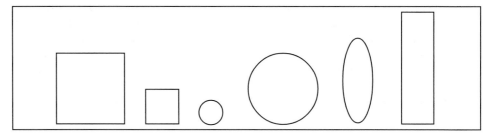

Figure 4.5 Halving shapes

Whichever way you completed this, the resulting halves will be discrete different shapes and/or sizes and yet they will all still be given the same symbol, ½! This doesn't happen with counting numbers. If there are four objects, whatever they may be, then they are counted and labelled '4' and not '6' or any other number! This indicates that just as providing children with experience of a wide range of different pairs of objects helps them to abstract the concept of 'twoness', so children must experience a range of objects and actions with the one common property of 'halfness' and halving.

Task 5

Ask some children to tell you what fraction is represented by the shaded portions in Figure 4.6.

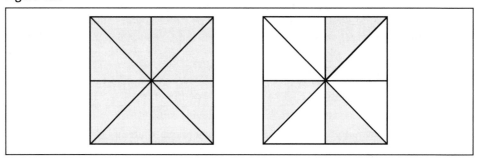

Figure 4.6 Recognising fractions

You may be surprised (or not!) to get answers of $\frac{11}{8}$ and $\frac{11}{16}$. There seems to be a reluctance to see fractions as greater than one, in this case $1\frac{3}{8}$, though $\frac{11}{8}$ is certainly acceptable mathematically.

Other 'real life' activities include halving and quartering biscuits, cakes, fruit or other foods. However, if children's images of fractions remain at this concrete level then adding, subtracting, multiplying and dividing half an apple to, from or by a quarter of a chocolate bar, will have no sensible meaning. In one Key Stage 1 SAT many children confidently and accurately shaded in a fraction of a shape but were thrown into confusion when a following question asked them to indicate the same fraction of a number. Teachers made sure that for the next SAT children understood that numbers too can be halved, quartered, etc.

So how do children perceive fractions? Children should be told that fractions are numbers in their own right and, as such, have specific operations defined on them. Unfortunately, the same words employed for operations on whole numbers are used to describe operations on fractions. It is therefore no wonder that many children are puzzled that what was marked correct before suddenly does not apply. Some teaching uses a hybrid symbol such as a ringed 'plus' $\oplus$ to highlight that another form of 'addition' applies for fractions.

It has already been discussed that children falling behind in maths are unappreciative of the dual nature of, or equivalences inherent in, mathematical symbols. More able children will be able to understand the symbol $\frac{3}{4}$, both as the concept of three-quarters of something (as well as the ratio 3 : 4), and the process 3 ÷ 4, and be able to call on whichever form is appropriate. Children who believe that a smaller number cannot be divided by a larger number and would rearrange the calculation to 4 ÷ 3 and give the result as 1 remainder 1, for example, do not have this facility. It is worth examining the language form you would use for the division, 3 ÷ 4. Would you say, for example, '4 into 3'; '3 share 4'; '3 shared by 4'; '4 divided into 3'; or some other phrase? Where did this come from? Do the phrases resonate with (common) sense? Children need to know that for numbers the correct term is 'something divided by something'.

Task 6
Read the section in the NNF on fractions (pp. 20–23, section 6).

 ## Decimals

Children need to be aware that decimals, along with percentages, are alternative ways of representing fractions. As before, the more successful children will be able to move freely between them, choosing the most appropriate for a given context. For example knowing that calculating $33\frac{1}{3}$% of a quantity is equivalent to finding $\frac{1}{3}$ of it, which itself is equivalent to dividing the quantity by 3, is another example of a 'lot for a little'. In this case, using its decimal equivalent of 0.3333... would involve a lot more work. It is therefore essential that common or useful fractions represented as points on the number line are also labelled with their decimal or percentage equivalents, as in Figure 4.7.

0%	25%	50%	75%	100%
0.00	0.25	0.50	0.75	1.00
0	$\frac{1}{4}$	$\frac{1}{2}$	$\frac{3}{4}$	1

Figure 4.7 A number line of common and useful fractions with their decimal or percentage equivalents

To emphasise and reinforce the fraction-decimal duality it is worth using the phrase 'decimal fractions' with children rather than just 'decimals'.

Children who have understood 'fractions' and the logic and notation of our place value system, in particular that dividing by ten forces each digit of a number one place to its immediate right, making it one-tenth of its previous value, will be better able to accommodate the extension of the notation for representing decimal numbers; including the idea that the decimal point is merely a convenient convention to distinguish its whole number part from its fraction part. Children who have little idea of the 'ten-ness' of a decimal number will show this by responses of 63, 603, six and a third and so on to the question: 'What does 6.3 mean?'.

Similarly those children who know that $\frac{3}{8}$ and $1\frac{3}{4}$, for example, can also be interpreted as 3 ÷ 8 and 7 ÷ 4, will be able to convert all fractions (or, more strictly, fraction notation or symbols) to their decimal form and, in many cases, back again.

Common misconceptions

For planning and diagnosis, it is worth knowing what common misconceptions children may carry in their understanding. For some, the decimal point has little meaning and so (quite naturally) they may try to make sense of a decimal number by locating it in their understanding of whole numbers. They may ignore the point to read 5.63 as 563 or even as the two numbers, 5 and 63. Such children will believe that 0.7 is smaller than 0.534. Others have been known to confuse the decimal point with other separators such as: the remainder 'r' in '8 r 1'; the dot in 3.25am; or the comma in a coordinate pair such as (4,6). Technology may also add to the confusion about the position of the point: above or on the line on which the numbers stand (depending on the typeface). Cycle computers often represent times with two points (as in 1.09.43 to represent one hour, nine minutes, and 43 seconds).

Money is often used as a context for teaching decimals. Unfortunately this can cause confusion when amounts such as £1.28 are commonly read and said as 'one twenty eight', or 'one pound twenty eight', thus reinforcing whole number perceptions as described above. Children who have problems with this can easily be identified by their misreading of a range of decimal numbers, or by their misinterpretation of a calculator display of say (£)0.8 as 'eight pence'. The latter example also indicates children who are confused about the role of zero as a place holder, at least in this context.

Responses of 'none' to the question: 'How many different numbers lie between 0.53 and 0.54?', for example, indicate that those children do not appreciate that an infinite number of decimals lie between any two given end points. Further work on representing numbers on the number line would help them to develop a supportive mental picture.

Finally, consider an approach described earlier, that of asking children to write a story for a given calculation. This can quickly give insight into children's understanding. For 4.3 + 5.6 =? one response was: 'Mary had 4.3 sweets and Joe had 5.6 sweets. They had 9.9 sweets altogether.' This shows (or does it?) that the child can add decimals without really understanding what is going on.

Task 7 (Optional)

Choose some of the ideas above and try them out with a group of Year 6 children (or even Year 7 if you have access). How do their responses compare with those suggested?
Unfortunately, many of the common algorithms used for operating on decimals hide the underlying mathematical structure and may lead to instrumental rather than relational understanding. These include exhortations like: 'line up the decimal points, fill any spaces with zeros, then proceed as though it were an 'ordinary' addition/subtraction.' Notice how the word 'ordinary' can imply that some trickery or something magical has taken place. Learned as a rule it becomes just one more unconnected fact to add to a child's memory, which is possibly already overloaded with other items, and subject to misinterpretation and/or forgetting, especially when the same rule is applied to multiplying decimals, for example.

You may be interested to know that the gelosia algorithm of multiplication (see pp. 33–34) can be used with decimals, though it takes some thought to understand why it works. Again, it is much easier to explain verbally than in writing! Using a slight variation of the earlier example, calculate 2.6 x 3.4 using Figure 4.8.

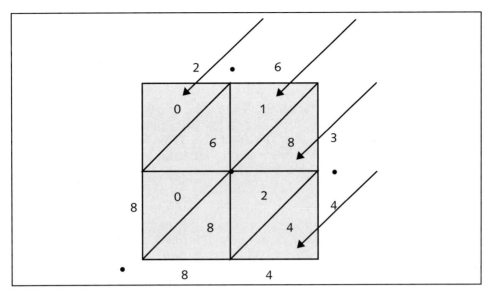

Figure 4.8 The gelosia method of multiplication using decimals

The result is calculated just as before. To determine the final position of the point, imagine each point from the 2.6 and the 3.4 to slide vertically down and horizontally to the left, respectively, merging into one at the centre of the diagram. Now imagine this sliding down the diagonal to finish at the position shown, giving the answer 8.84. Again this reeks of magic, but then so does the algorithm: 'forget the point, treat the calculation as you would for whole numbers. Now count up the places after the decimal point in the original sum and put one that many places to the right in your answer.'

A more relational approach could be to perform the multiplication, ignoring the points, as though whole numbers were being used, giving 884. Returning to the original problem you might note that rounding 2.6 to 3 and 3.4 to 3 would give an approximated product of 9. Inspecting 884 it would seem sensible to place the point to give 8.84.

Another approach demonstrating the mathematics behind it is that of multiplying and dividing by powers of ten and doubling as appropriate: For 53.82 x 9.318 (a little extreme perhaps, but it does show the structure!):

53.82	**9.138**
100	913.8
50	**456.9**
1	9.138
2	18.276
3	**27.414**
.2	1.8276
.4	3.6552
.8	**7.3104**
.02	0.18276
53.82	491.80716

Task 8
Read the section in the NNF on fractions and decimals (pp. 28–33, section 6).

Approximating and estimating

Children should know methods of confirming that, whatever operation they have used, their answers are of the right order of magnitude. One of the current concerns of the National Curriculum and the NNS is that children can make sensible approximations of numbers and operate on these to give estimates of exact answers (see the example for 2.6 x 3.4, in Task 7). Thus children will need to practise rounding numbers to the nearest whole number, ten, or other power of ten (100, 1,000, 10,000, etc.), depending on their developmental stage. This may be facilitated by them placing numbers between significant end points on an appropriate number line.

 Percentages

Task 9

Without using a calculator, examine the method(s) you would use to work out the VAT (at $17\frac{1}{2}$%) applied to an article whose pre-VAT price is £136.

Whichever way you performed this calculation it is important to be aware that, though some methods may be more efficient than others (and perhaps only for you), there is no single correct approach. The National Curriculum (Key Stage 2, Ma2, Level 4) expects children to use 'simple' percentages and fractions to represent proportions of a whole, with calculations involving them not specifically addressed until Levels 5 and 6, where calculator-based methods are also acceptable. (Pie charts, a common context for calculating and displaying percentages, are similarly a feature of attainment at Level 5 in Ma4.)

However, many resourceful children can make use of the *ad hoc* methods described earlier to calculate percentages of quantities at least and the current VAT rate of $17\frac{1}{2}$% is well suited to a halving technique:

> 10% of £136 is £13.60
> 5% of £136 is £6.80
> $2\frac{1}{2}$% of £136 is £3.40
> $17\frac{1}{2}$% of £136 is £ 23.80

> The VAT-inclusive price is £159.80

Compare the structure clearly evident in this approach with that of the clerk you met back on p. 3. (By the way did you work out why the clerk multiplied by the factor of 0.851? Perhaps as follows? Considering the VAT-exclusive price as 100%, then the VAT-inclusive price is $117\frac{1}{2}$% of the original. To find 1% of the original, divide the VAT-inclusive price by $117\frac{1}{2}$. To find 100% multiply this result by 100. Dividing by $117\frac{1}{2}$ followed by multiplying by 100 is equivalent to multiplying by 0.851 (3 decimal places). Applying this to £159.80, above:

£159.80 x 0.851 = £135.99 (£136 to the nearest penny)

No wonder the clerk is content just to multiply by 0.851! (But how difficult would this be if a calculator were not available.)

Section 7 Algebra objectives

By the end of this section you will:
- have reviewed your knowledge of algebra;
- be aware that the underlying structures of number are algebraic in nature;
- have an understanding of the knowledge, skills and understanding required of progressive levels;
- be aware of a range of activities and contexts encompassing the requirements.

So far we have looked at number only and you may be wondering where the algebra comes in. A quick look at AT2 (Attainment Target 2) will show you that x itself is not mentioned until Level 6! However, as has been said before, it is very important that children learn that there are underlying patterns in mathematics which can be used to gain a 'lot from a little'. For example, the idea of equivalence means that knowing 3 x 4 = 12 allows us to use several alternative forms of the numbers and operation. The activities you provide which encompass these underlying structures and patterns are really what algebra is all about.

We have previously discussed the laws of commutativity and distributivity, as these are essential for allowing us to make equivalences. For completeness we need to consider a third fundamental law of arithmetic and algebra, that of associativity. An example will make this clear:

How would you tackle 3 x 4 x 5?

You might have paired and multiplied the numbers from left to right, i.e. (3 x 4) before multiplying the result by 5 to obtain 60.

Alternatively, you might have paired the numbers this way, (3 x 5) x 4 and still got 60. Again, possibly most conveniently for a child, you might have paired (4 x 5) x 3 = 60. Whichever way you performed the multiplication, the answer is constant. The associative law says just that: for three or more numbers it doesn't matter which pair you multiply first, the final answer is constant.

Task 10
Read pp. 9–10 of the introduction to NNS. This specifies and lists in more detail the interrelationship between number and algebra. For each of the headings given, identify appropriate activities and National Curriculum Levels, and complete the table in Figure 4.9.

Algebra	Early algebraic activities	National Curriculum Level
Forming equations		
Solving equations		
Using inverses		
Identifing number patterns		
Expressing relationships		
Drawing graphs		
Developing ideas of continuity		
Finding equivalent forms		
Factorising numbers		
Understanding the commutative, associative and distributive laws		

Figure 4.9 Laying the foundations for algebra

Chapter 5

Ma3: Shape, space and measures

Objectives

By the end of this chapter you will have:

- gained an overview of the requirements of this section;

- determined a range of activities appropriate to, and beyond, your placements;

- become aware of the place of shape, space and measures (SSM) in the maths curriculum and other curricular areas;

- been introduced to some common misconceptions in children's understanding of this section;

- reviewed your own knowledge of standard units and the relationships between them.

In the National Curriculum, the section on SSM clearly indicates the requirement for children to develop their understanding of shape, space and measures via practical, tactile and purposeful activities. It indicates the importance of children using associated vocabulary and language appropriate to their stage of development to help them to construct their understanding. Teaching the specified content for this section will enable you to help children to explore and become aware of the rich and inevitable interconnections between shape, space and measures. However, for planning and assessment purposes subsections 2 and 3 of the National Curriculum focus on shape and space, with subsection 4 devoted to measures.

 Shape and space

First it is very important to be aware that the inclusion of 'space' in the title of this section means that all children must study the properties of 3-dimensional shapes as well as those represented in print which by its nature can only be 1- or 2-dimensional. In practice this can often be done concurrently – a solid object such as a cube (3D) can be described in terms of its six square faces (2D), or its twelve straight edges (1D), for example.

It is at times difficult to make an absolute distinction between the National Curriculum content listed in Ma3(2) 'Understanding patterns and properties of shape' and Ma3(3) 'Understanding properties of position and movement' and consequently the assessment of children's achievement in these.

Figures 5.1 and 5.2 show a developmental sequence of activities involving both 3D and 2D shapes aimed approximately at children aged 7–9 (Deboys and Pitt 1993). Alongside each activity is a brief description of what it involves together with some appropriate question or instruction aimed at offering a challenging context for children to explore.

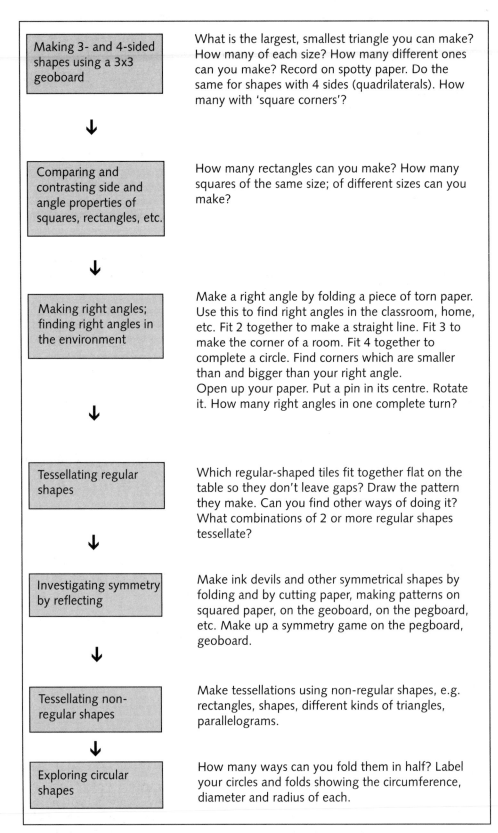

Making 3- and 4-sided shapes using a 3x3 geoboard	What is the largest, smallest triangle you can make? How many of each size? How many different ones can you make? Record on spotty paper. Do the same for shapes with 4 sides (quadrilaterals). How many with 'square corners'?
↓	
Comparing and contrasting side and angle properties of squares, rectangles, etc.	How many rectangles can you make? How many squares of the same size; of different sizes can you make?
↓	
Making right angles; finding right angles in the environment	Make a right angle by folding a piece of torn paper. Use this to find right angles in the classroom, home, etc. Fit 2 together to make a straight line. Fit 3 to make the corner of a room. Fit 4 together to complete a circle. Find corners which are smaller than and bigger than your right angle. Open up your paper. Put a pin in its centre. Rotate it. How many right angles in one complete turn?
↓	
Tessellating regular shapes	Which regular-shaped tiles fit together flat on the table so they don't leave gaps? Draw the pattern they make. Can you find other ways of doing it? What combinations of 2 or more regular shapes tessellate?
↓	
Investigating symmetry by reflecting	Make ink devils and other symmetrical shapes by folding and by cutting paper, making patterns on squared paper, on the geoboard, on the pegboard, etc. Make up a symmetry game on the pegboard, geoboard.
↓	
Tessellating non-regular shapes	Make tessellations using non-regular shapes, e.g. rectangles, shapes, different kinds of triangles, parallelograms.
↓	
Exploring circular shapes	How many ways can you fold them in half? Label your circles and folds showing the circumference, diameter and radius of each.

Figure 5.1 2D: Suggested progression and activities (Deboys and Pitt 1993)

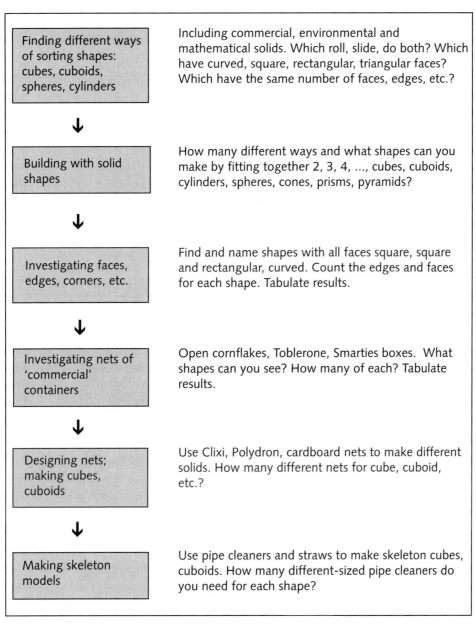

Figure 5.2 3D: Suggested progression and activities (Deboys and Pitt 1993)

Task 1
Work through as many of the activities as you can yourself. Make notes of any specific vocabulary you needed to use to record your results.

Task 2
For the class you are teaching identify the range of levels the children are working at in Ma3. Identify the appropriate statements for these levels. Using any school or LEA guidance, the NNS and your own imagination, describe one activity which you could use to enable children to demonstrate attainment for each of the statements you've listed. Explain how and why the activities address the statements. You can record your findings in Figure 5.3.

Level	Name of Child(ren)	Activity which demonstrated attainment at this level
1		
2		
3		
4		
5		
6		

Figure 5.3 Identifying Levels in Ma3

 **Measures**

Task 3

Carry out several of these or similar measurements. As you do so, describe and list your actions, including making a note of any related vocabulary:

- a piece of material to use as a tablecloth (what if the table were circular?);
- a piece of card to make a box to hold a block of ice cream;
- a quantity of liquid to add to a recipe;
- a bag of pick-and-mix sweets;
- how long to make a journey;
- the bearing of some prominent point on a map.

Although the attributes measured – length, area, capacity, volume, mass (weight), time and angle – are different, for each act of measuring you would have essentially:

- seen some point in why you were measuring;
- chosen an appropriate unit or 'tool';
- compared this with the object to be measured;
- counted the number of times the unit is required to 'fill' or 'cover' the object.

Here again we have 'a lot for a little'. Imagine if you had to learn a different technique of measuring depending on the object being measured! The interrelationships are nicely summarised in Figure 5.4.

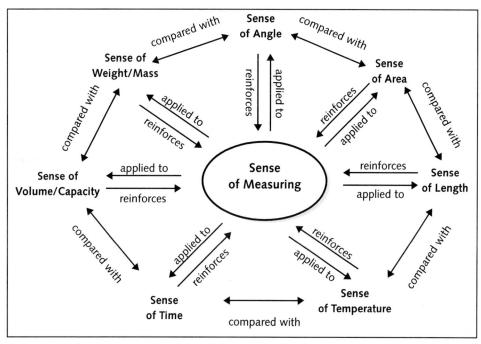

Figure 5.4 The Sense of Measuring (Open University 1996, p. 103)

To develop this sense of measurement, children's learning is usually structured through the three stages listed below (Deboys and Pitt 1993) and mediated through appropriate language.

1. Pre-measuring: comparing two or more objects;
    ordering three or more objects;
    equivalence of two objects;
    conservation experiences.
2. Using arbitrary units.
3. Using standard units.

Task 4
Read the NNF sections on measures in section 4 (pp. 22 and 23), section 5 (pp. 72–79) and section 6 (pp. 92–101).
Ask for help if there is anything you do not understand.

 The approximate nature of measuring; the precise nature of measures

The principle of transitivity is fundamental. For example, the relationship 'is equal to', enables us to ensure that a shop-bought kitchen cabinet will fit along a wall without having to take the wall to the shop! Transitivity in this case means that because the length of the wall is equal to the length of the ruler or tape measure, which itself is equal to that of the cabinet, then the wall length is the same as that of the cabinet.

The difference between mass and weight, for example, is hindered by everyday language and can cause difficulty. Children will, therefore, also need much practice in using the logic, language and conversion factors of the Système Internationale (SI) system. However, textbook exercises of addition and subtraction can often be translated into scientific activity, thus killing two birds with one stone by giving them some point and meaning.

Perhaps even more than these, children will need to become aware of the approximate nature of the act of measuring itself: the degree of accuracy quoted, needed or is implicit depends on the preciseness of the instrument used. They therefore need to be encouraged to make estimates in a variety of units and contexts, both arbitrary and standard, imperial and metric, before any act of measuring. These, including as Haylock (2001) suggests, the use of parts of their own bodies as portable measuring instruments, and rhymes will help to familiarise them with the units themselves and the relationships between them. In contrast, children will also need to learn that when measures are expressed in, or converted to, different units, the relationship or conversion factor between them is exact – 1000mm can be expressed as 100cm, 1m or 0.001km, for example.

The act of measuring raises children's awareness of the need for a vocabulary to describe the 'extra' or 'not quite' bits, over or under the unit or tool being used, and they will become aware of the need for symbols to represent these fractional parts to record and communicate their measurements. Conventional fraction and decimal notation should not be introduced too quickly and without reference to the concrete activities which should precede it.

Consequently the context of measuring provides a major vehicle for children to develop their understanding of the ideas and language of approximating and estimating, as well as operations on fractions, especially decimal fractions, to help them to avoid the misconceptions described in Chapter 4.

The paragraph above clearly shows the artificiality and impossibility of considering each section of the National Curriculum as a separate discrete entity. Using the context of one can help to promote understanding in another and you have already seen how the classification of shapes can assist in early concept-forming. Similarly, the tessellating property of squares and cubes in filling surfaces and space leads to measures of area and volume. Using shapes to build patterns and spatially arranging a number of objects into rectangular, square and triangular arrays gives concrete representations of some underlying structures of number and algebra.

Similarly to his progression for shape and space, Pinel (1992) has also helpfully identified the National Curriculum developmental sequence for measures:

Level

1   comparing and ordering objects and events without measuring, using appropriate language
2   understanding the conservation of length, capacity, mass ('weight'), etc.
4   finding perimeters of simple shapes
    finding areas by counting squares and volumes by counting cubes
5   measuring and drawing angles to the nearest degree
    finding the areas of plane (i.e. 2D) figures, excluding circles using appropriate formulae
    finding volumes of simple solids (i.e. 3D), excluding cylinders using appropriate formulae
    finding the circumference of circles practically, introducing the ratio π
6   finding areas of circles using the formula.

Common misconceptions

It is useful to be aware of, and plan for, some common misconceptions. These are generally held by older children, though presumably developed from inappropriate experiences at an earlier age. For example, children who are almost always presented with geometric figures, such as polygons which are regular (i.e. having all sides and angles equal) and stand on a horizontal base, are unlikely to recognise the shapes in the orientations in Figure 5.5 as a square, triangle and hexagon.

Children's stereotypical images need to be challenged by you presenting and discussing with them a wide variety of shapes in different orientations, asking questions like: 'If I move or turn this, what changes and what stays the same?'

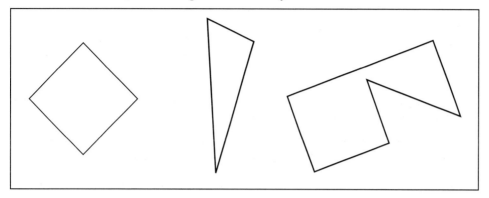

Figure 5.5 Recognising geometric shapes

The case of angle is worth a special mention: it can be considered as the point created by the intersection of two straight lines (static) or, more usefully, as the amount of turn from one position to another, clockwise or anticlockwise (dynamic).

Some children have little understanding of angle as a measure of turn and this is evidenced by those who believe that of the two representations of the same angle in Figure 5.6, B is bigger. These children may be seeing the size of an angle in terms of the length of its arms or the area enclosed by the arms.

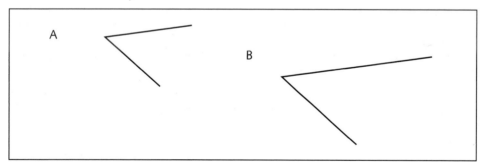

Figure 5.6 Two representations of the same angle

Some children will only see lines as meeting at right angles if they are presented as A, in Figure 5.7. They find difficulty in accepting the representation shown in B.

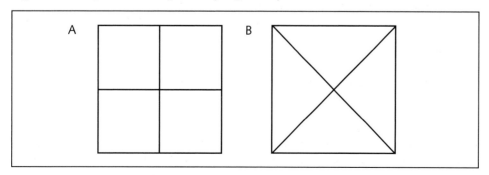

Figure 5.7 Recognising right angles

Similarly many children have a limited understanding of the concepts of 'horizontal', 'vertical', and especially 'parallel' if the lines are presented as sloping, as shown in Figure 5.8.

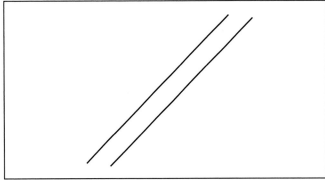

Figure 5.8 Grasping the concept of 'horizontal', 'vertical' and 'parallel' in sloping lines

 ## Making links with other parts of the curriculum

Beyond 'pure' mathematics, other curriculum areas may exploit both the static and dynamic aspects of this section to enrich children's experience:
- in art, the aesthetic pleasure to be found in constructing various symmetries of patterns and designs resides in their mathematical properties;
- in science, children can investigate the properties of shapes in the natural world and offer reasons why they might have evolved this way;
- in geography, ideas of scale can help children to specify the location and distance of a place on an A–Z or more complex map;
- in history, children can construct pyramids and learn to marvel at how the Egyptians managed to build theirs with little more than knotted string and other rudimentary tools;
- in PE, children can explore their place in the space around them using free or structured turns and other movements, as in dance steps.

In short, if you as a teacher are aware of all these, and more, links with maths you will be able to draw on their potential as trigger questions to help children to see the interconnections between them and hence aid their relational understanding:

'Remember when we did full and quarter turns in PE?'

'Tell me again how you made that lovely pattern (by sliding, reflecting, rotating a shape).'

'Pretend you're an Egyptian. Show me how you used that string to make a right angle/draw a circle.'

'Give me some of your favourite places to find on this A–Z.'

and so on.

Task 5

Read pp. 16 and 17 of the introduction to the NNF. This gives some good ideas for making links between mathematics and other subjects. Many of these activities can be linked to measures.

There can be a temptation to omit some (admittedly messy) practical activities, not because you don't value them (though this of course may be the case) but because at a particular time the organisational requirements may seem daunting. It may seem as effective, and much easier, just to give children (older children especially) the names of shapes first, followed by a list of defining properties. While there is no denying that this can be a very efficient mode of knowledge transmission, such definitions usually depend on a hierarchy of previously-understood concepts.

If you are teaching children whose understanding of 'parallel' and 'angle', for example, matches those described above, then it is unlikely that, without a lot of extra questioning and work on both your parts, they will be able to fit the ideas associated with any new names into their existing understanding. These may become yet more fragmented facts, subject to loss or misinterpretation.

Chapter 6

Ma4: Handling data

Objectives

By the end of this chapter you will:

- have reviewed and revised your own knowledge, skills and understanding of data handling and probability including the difference between discrete and continuous data;
- have an understanding of the requirements of this section;
- be aware of the cyclic nature of the data-handling process;
- be familiar with and recognise progression in a variety of ways of representing data;
- have reviewed your knowledge of electronic databases.

This chapter consists of two strands: collecting, representing and interpreting data; understanding and using probability.

The first thing you should do is review your own subject knowledge of the former.

 The data-handling cycle

Task 1

Read through the relevant part of the programme of study (Ma4) in the National Curriculum document.

Figure 6.1 is an amended version of Haylock's (2001) linear 4-stage process. This has been changed to a cyclical model to include the very important point he makes that children should collect, organise, represent and interpret data in order to answer some purposeful enquiry or problem of their own.

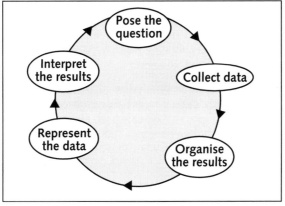

Figure 6.1 Model of the data-handling cycle

Some non-mathematical contexts seem naturally to generate questions which may be particularly motivating for children. For example, they may ask in:
- PE – 'Do people with longer legs run the fastest?';

- science – 'What sort of balls are bounciest?';

- history – 'What sort of jobs did children do in this period of time?';

- geography – 'Where did the people who worked in this factory come from?';

- music/drama – 'What sort of presentation would parents like this year?'

These questions are 'open' in the sense that they give children a chance to decide what is important to them in terms of the evidence needed, how best to find this out, and how to interpret their findings in the light of why they wanted to know in the first place. (However, you will need to be sensitive to the fact that some of the contexts commonly used for children to generate data, comparing body proportions or family circumstances for example, may be a source of embarrassment.)

In tackling general queries like the ones above, children will need to discuss and agree on:
- what will constitute relevant data (e.g. what is meant by 'longer');

- a mechanism for collecting it (e.g. a questionnaire for primary data, that which they collect themselves; or secondary data, that from a published source);

- who or what to include or exclude (i.e. a sample and size);

- the most appropriate way of representing or displaying their data (an electronic database may present them with a novel approach);

- the degree to which the data answers the original question;

- whether further investigation is needed.

Compare this with the requirements of a much more specific and 'closed' task, for example asking a class to record and display 'Our favourite animals'. Of course, one aim here might be to check that the class can perform some related technique, such as making a block graph or drawing a bar chart. But even with this, rehearsing a technique provides an opportunity for children to start thinking about their results. Depending on their attainment, children might be asked: 'What can you tell me from your chart?', encouraging them to go beyond a response of 'Most children like chimps', by asking why they think this is so. 'Would the results be the same if we included some other animals?' 'Is the same true for other classes in our school?'

An even better approach would be to ask a more open question in the first place: 'I read that cats are most people's favourite animal. Why do you think this is? How could we find out?'

This focus on the interpretive aspect of data handling rather than its mechanical representation is made all the more important by the availability and ease of use of the chart-plotting and drawing capabilities of the computer databases available in schools, even for the youngest of children. These offer the potential of visually exciting and almost instantaneous displays and children might consider various representations of the same data and choose the one (or more) most appropriate to their needs. Before computers (BC!) it was difficult to give children entry to anything but small samples of primary data and managing this, especially if modifications were required, was never easy. Computer databases enable children to access both primary and secondary sources, make hypotheses and test these against what may be a large amount of stored information.

For example, a group of Year 4 children trying to decide who was the best 'guesser' began their investigation by defining the essential qualities needed to be good at guessing. This led to them devising a range of activities – from estimating how many sweets could be grabbed in a handful to estimating how far a 'tiddly' could be 'winked'. As the majority of tasks required measurement this led them to specify degrees of accuracy. They were then able to enter each child's results onto a database (in this case *Junior Pinpoint*) and find, for instance, who was above or below the average which was quickly calculated by the database. They were able to use the chart-drawing facility to produce and print graphs and pie charts and talk knowledgeably about their findings. This was most noticeable in their use of scatter graphs to see if there was any correlation between being good at guessing in different contexts.

Task 2

The NNS lists key objectives for each of the years Reception to Year 6. For each year group, identify those which relate specifically to data handling. Make a note of any National Curriculum items that are not covered by the NNS.

Task 3

Identify and familiarise yourself with the database(s) used in your school. Make sure you know how to enter data and interrogate it appropriately. Observe or find out how children learn to use them.

Various approaches may be used, ranging from the teacher giving a demonstration to a group; knowledgeable children teaching their peers; giving individual instruction or free exploration (see Chapter 8). Your school's approach might mean that children may be using a mathematical context to help them learn about databases or using databases to help them learn mathematics. You will need to be clear about which approach is being used, not least for assessment and recording purposes. Schools with computer suites and/ or interactive whiteboards may use these facilities for some very effective direct teaching.

② Representing data

It is important, as was pointed out in Chapter 2, to remember that the classifying aspect of handling data, amongst others, is subsumed within Ma2 Number for Key Stage 1. The sorting and classifying activity of young children, as was described earlier, is a precursor to more formal data handling, as well as ideas of shape, space and number. Sorting sets of objects into boxes or other containers, or more formally by placing them inside intersecting hoops or pre-drawn outlines as Venn and Carroll diagrams (Figure 6.2) is a Level 1 activity.

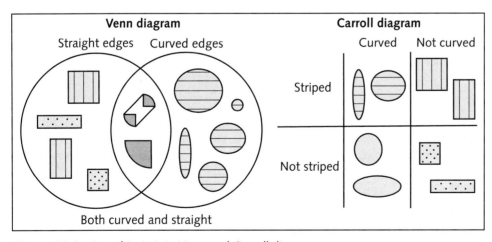

Figure 6.2 Sorting objects into Venn and Carroll diagrams

Early awareness (Level 1) of graphical representation can be raised by children sorting the objects themselves into columns and rows (Figure 6.3) which can then be compared visually to answer questions about which objects there are 'more of', 'fewer of', 'the same as', and so on. The need for a common baseline to ensure a fair comparison should be pointed out, if necessary.

Figure 6.3 Graphical representation of data in columns and rows

Level 2 begins the move away from concrete representation towards the more abstract notion of block graphs, as shown in Figure 6.4. So, for example, pictures of objects mounted on standard-sized cards (simple pictograms) can also be sorted, placed in columns and rows and similar questions asked. (Note: with respect to grouping data, pictograms feature at Level 3.)

Turning the rectangles over will maintain the structure of the graph and children can be encouraged to label each column with a picture of the object 'to help people who don't know what the rectangles represent'. The addition of a scale will also 'save us having to count each time'.

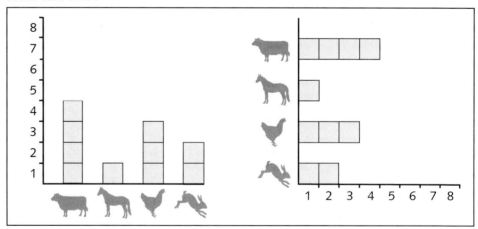

Figure 6.4 Block graphs

Alternative representations using simple frequency tables and mapping diagrams (Figure 6.5) can be made and the relative merits discussed.

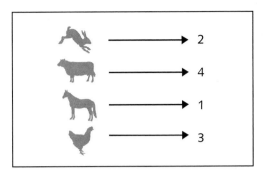

Figure 6.5 Mapping diagram

The condition of one-to-one correspondence for Levels 1 and 2 begins to develop with ideas of scaling, and the simultaneous introduction at Level 3 of the difference between discrete and continuous data. Because the 'chart' representations of these are similar, children may find it useful to leave gaps between bars representing discrete data and none between bars of frequency diagrams (see Figures 6.6 and 6.7).

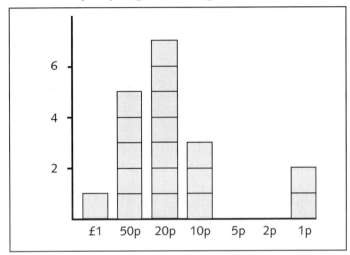

Figure 6.6 Bar chart to show coins in my pocket

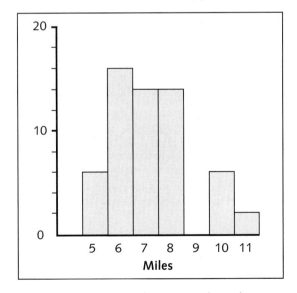

Figure 6.7 Frequency diagram to show distances achieved in a sponsored skateboard event

At this level, the number of data items is usually sufficiently small to be handled by a frequency table of the complexity shown in Figure 6.8:

Miles	Tally	Frequency
5	// ////	6
6	//// /// ////// // / /	16
7	////////////	14
8	////////////	14
9		0
10	/////	5
11	/	1

Figure 6.8 Frequency table to show distances achieved in a sponsored skateboard event

However, at Level 4, the 'five-barred gate' frequency table in Figure 6.9 is usually more convenient to record increasing amounts of data and the increasing need to consider it in groups.

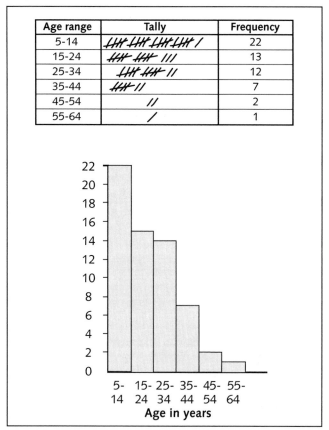

Age range	Tally	Frequency
5-14	✦✦✦✦ /	22
15-24	✦✦ ///	13
25-34	✦✦ //	12
35-44	✦//	7
45-54	//	2
55-64	/	1

Figure 6.9 Frequency table and diagram to show the age at which a group of people began smoking

Other representations at this level include bar-line graphs (Figure 6.10), useful when space is at a premium (perhaps for showing several temperature readings for each day of the week) and as a developmental link to line graphs.

The tops of bar-line graphs can be joined by straight lines, such as in Figure 6.11, but children need to understand that this may merely indicate a trend (like the fluctuation of daily temperatures) rather than providing a way to read off meaningful intermediate points.

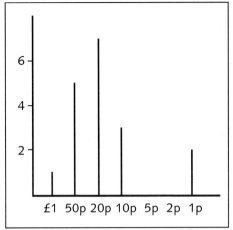

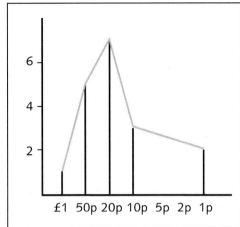

Figure 6.10 Bar-line graph to show coins in my pocket

Figure 6.11 Bar-line graph (with joined lines) to show coins in my pocket

Compare this with the graph in Figure 6.12 where intermediate values 'make sense' because the data is continuous.

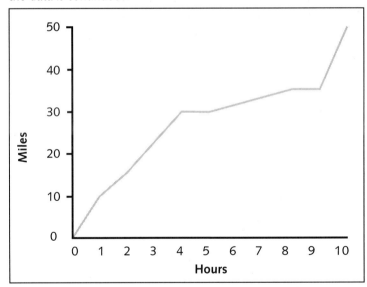

Figure 6.12 Line graph representing continuous data

For example, from the graph it is possible to estimate how many miles had been covered in $4\frac{1}{2}$ hours. Similarly it is possible to estimate how many hours it took to travel 32 miles.

As well as visual representation, Level 4 also introduces numerical summaries of a set of data. These are the mean, median and modal averages and, as well as being able to calculate these, children will need to be able to choose the most appropriate for a given context. Similarly the range, the difference between the lowest and highest value of the data, acts as a second descriptor when comparing two sets of data, especially if they have the same mean.

Care must be taken that children are not set the task of calculating averages only for the sake of it. Wherever possible these must be related to interpreting the context that they represent. If, however, you need them to practise the calculating skills required then why not set them more open and challenging tasks? 'Find three numbers that have, simultaneously, a median of 10, a mean of 8 and a range of 8. Can you find any more?'; 'Find four different numbers with a simultaneous mean of 12, mode of 6 and median of 7. Can you find more?'

Finally, it is important to point out that while children working at Level 5 are expected to interpret pie charts, the ability to construct them is a Level 6 requirement.

 Probability

Task 4
Review your understanding of the subject by reading NNF, section 6 pp. 112–113.

Probability is a means of describing and explaining unpredictable events, things which may or may not happen, and children need to become aware of several key ideas which underpin probability. The most important of these are *randomness* (as shown in the Lottery, where the outcomes of the event are wholly unpredictable) and *fairness* (where the *chance* of each of the 49 numbered balls being drawn is *equally likely*). If one ball were different, perhaps heavier than the others, then it *might* have *more chance* of being selected. Being *biased*, the draw would be *unfair* and not *random*.

Some of the previously italicised words indicate that *degrees of certainty* exist. At either extreme it is *impossible* to draw a ball numbered 33.3, for example, though it is *certain* that the balls drawn will be any of the numbers 1–49. In between these limits are conditions which are *more* or *less likely* to happen than others.

To quantify this spectrum of outcomes, and to give a measure of the likelihood of an event happening, the convention is to ascribe it a number, called its probability, between 0 (impossibility) and 1 (certainty). Most probabilities are therefore expressed as fractions less than 1, or their decimal or percentage equivalents. This means that if an event has a 40 per cent chance of happening it simultaneously has a 60 per cent chance of not happening.

While Level 4 attainment is measured in terms of children using the language associated with probability (as italicised above) Level 5 is concerned with using the scale to represent probabilities found by experiment (perhaps the relative frequency of the number of sixes occurring in 100 throws of a dice), and symmetry (for a fair dice, 6 is as likely to occur as any of the other numbers 1–5, so its probability is one in six or $\frac{1}{6}$. Can you now see why theoretically a 6 should occur about 16 or 17 times in 100 throws?).

Calculating with probabilities is seen as a skill for Level 6 and beyond. However, children need to understand that this is not just an esoteric branch of mathematics, it is part of their everyday lives (and not just on National Lottery nights!). It is not specifically addressed at Key Stage 1 (although it used to be) but as part of shared human experience even very young children will describe probability.

Task 5

Identify and record one or more moments in the past 24 hours when you have had cause to think about, or even calculate, probability outside of school (excluding the Lottery!). 'The traffic lights always seem to be on red when I'm in a hurry' or 'I wonder if that pedestrian is going to step out in front of me' are just two examples of when you might have to estimate chance or probability. The action you choose to take will depend on your experience of traffic lights and pedestrians. 'I caught an earlier train just in case I was late' and so on. Other examples might include: 'When I drop a piece of toast at breakfast it always falls buttered side down!' (Children love modelling this!)

Commonplaces such as: 'Red sky at night, shepherds' delight; red sky in the morning, shepherds' warning' are well-known predictions of the probability of, in this case, fine or bad weather prospects. How might you ask children to test this?

This type of saying (jot down any others which come to mind) indicate that humans have an intuitive grasp of probability and this can be nurtured indirectly in young children as a basis for later, more formal treatments. Classroom stories are an ideal context for this, especially for developing the language of probability. Children could, for example, act out a story such as *Katie Morag Delivers the Mail* (by Mairi Hedderwick 1997, Red Fox) where Katie Morag's offer to deliver five parcels is hampered by her falling in a pool so that all the names on the parcels are too smudged to read. She only knows Grannie's because it has a red label. What are Grannie's chances of getting the right parcel? What about the others? The contents of the parcels are unknown until after they have been delivered and children can be encouraged to predict and justify what might be in the next parcel as each is opened. Why do they think that? Repeating this will encourage them to realise that for all the parcels, apart from Grannie's, there may be several different outcomes.

Task 6 (Optional)

From a range of books which your class is reading, identify which might be used to reinforce ideas of probability. List some questions you could ask to elicit understanding. (Note: You don't have to stick to probability – *Flat Stanley* (by Jeff Brown 1989, Mammoth) can be used as a basis for work on area.)

Chapter 7

Using and applying mathematics

Objectives

By the end of this chapter you will have:

- gained an overview of the requirements of Ma1 Using and applying mathematics;
- experienced a range of activities appropriate to and beyond your placements;
- become aware of the fundamental place of Using and Applying in the mathematics curriculum;
- gained an understanding of how progression develops.

 ## 'They understand how to multiply but not when to multiply.'

This teacher's frustration is often paralleled by children's own when, for example, after successfully completing a page of 'mechanical' calculations, they are faced with a page of 'problems'. You may remember that Chapter 4 discussed an instance of this where the wording of a question can mean the difference between success and failure.

Many adults have reported a sinking feeling as they approached the 'problem page'. So much so that their speed of working on the 'mechanical' questions was adjusted in order to avoid facing this! This occurred even though they knew that the problems usually encompassed the algorithms which they had just completed successfully.

The introduction of the National Curriculum in 1988 made statutory this aspect of teaching mathematics which previously was at best implicit and at worst ignored. In particular this was not assessed directly in public examinations, as it currently is in GCSE, for example, by means of coursework. Prior to the introduction of this, Cockcroft (DES 1982) had famously listed six 'elements which need to be present in successful mathematics teaching to pupils of all ages'. These include:

- exposition by the teacher;
- discussion between teacher and pupils and pupils themselves;
- practical work;
- consolidation and practice of fundamental routines;
- problem solving, including those of 'everyday' situations;
- investigational work.

These are discussed in more detail in paragraphs 244–253 of the Cockcroft Report (DES 1982), which is still well worth reading.

This promoting of a large part of mathematics learning as an active social process for children has helped to dispel the perception (though not necessarily the practice) of children as passive and lone problem solvers. One of the reasons why children may have found problems difficult is that they were not directly taught any strategies to solve them and were expected to find the answer (usually contained in the question) for themselves.

Assessment

Another, more pragmatic, reason is that assessing just how, and how well, children are using and applying their mathematics was difficult – even with a hierarchy of criteria specified. This presents teachers and children with the most significant challenge within the maths curriculum. On the positive side, it does become easier with experience.

Task 1

Find out and make notes on how AT1 (Ma1 Using and applying mathematics) is assessed in your school. You will probably find it most useful to ask the subject coordinator.
This may depend to some extent upon initiatives of LEAs. For example, geographical clusters of schools may be established where teachers are invited periodically to moderate their assessments of aspects of children's work from across all the curriculum. A similar process within each school may have preceded this.

While it seems self-evident that the characteristics of Ma1 permeate the whole of the maths curriculum, the difficulties outlined above seem to have generated two approaches to its teaching, learning and assessment, neither of which should be seen as mutually exclusive. One approach translates Cockcroft's idea of 'investigational work' into periodic set tasks, 'investigations', separated from 'normal' maths activity. The teacher's primary focus here is on the strategies that children bring to the problem, and is as far as possible independent of the content of the area of maths itself. For many teachers this has been, and continues to be, their route into giving children an understanding of the requirements of Ma1. 'Problem Solving' can also fall into this trap.

Exclusive use of this method may be criticised as being an 'add-on' rather than fulfilling the spirit of Ma1. However, many investigations, rather than being used as isolated discrete tasks, can be used as motivating challenges to introduce or reinforce a topic, and children's findings can provide a useful concrete reference for the more formal teaching which may follow ('Do you remember how you explained this when you were working on...?').

This technique is a kind of halfway house between the different perspectives of 'investigations' (as just another topic to be taught, much like fractions or volume), and 'investigating' (where the strategies used in investigations are applied as the underlying principle of teaching and learning the majority of the maths curriculum).

Task 2

Re-read the sections on mathematical development in the *Curriculum Guidance for the foundation stage* **(QCA/DfEE 2000) pp. 68–73. Many, if not most, of the activities here are 'investigations'.**

Strategies

At this point it will be useful for you to get some sense of what is involved in investigating by attempting an investigation for yourself and considering the strategies required. As you work through it, note down any strategies you use, especially those you fall back on if you become stuck.

Task 3

How many squares are there on a chessboard?
You may find it useful to have a chessboard to hand! (Experience indicates that some children do not know that a chessboard and draughts board are the same.) At first glance you will realise that the simple answer of 64 is too trivial and that there may be more to it. Further reflection may encourage you to increase this to 65 by including the 8 x 8 square encompassing the board. This, in turn, may help you to see the board as being made up of a collection of 1 x 1, 2 x 2, 3 x 3, 4 x 4, 5 x 5, 6 x 6, 7 x 7 and 8 x 8 squares. At this point you will need some strategy to ensure that none of these squares is missing from your count. A useful technique is to tabulate your results – if you begin this with the number of 8 x 8 squares you might soon be able to see a pattern:

8 x 8	1
7 x 7	4
6 x 6	9
5 x 5	16
4 x 4	25
3 x 3	
2 x 2	
1 x 1	
Total	**204**

Can you complete it?

Task 4

Compare your actions with the level descriptions listed in AT1. Can you translate between them easily? Did you, for example, predict how many and test your conjecture?
You may have used this strategy:

- understand the problem;
- devise a plan;
- carry it out;
- review and check.

Secondary maths departments often give children a more detailed hierarchical list of instructions or guidelines to refer to when they are doing an investigation. This aims at ensuring that they cover all the attributes required of Ma1 or GCSE coursework. By and large this does not seem to happen in primary schools.

 Problems and Investigations

You may by now be wondering what actually constitutes the difference between a problem and an investigation.

Task 5

Write down the differences and similarities you see, if any, between a 'problem' and an 'investigation'.

The chessboard activity in Task 3 can probably be considered as problem solving as you were encouraged to find a solution and no more. If you were to develop the initial question, open it up for further speculation (perhaps by considering chessboards of different sizes – 10 x 10, 100 x 100, n x n) then you might be considered to be investigating. You might further speculate and investigate how many rectangles there are on chessboards of various sizes. What about the number of triangles in a triangular chessboard? Moving into three dimensions you could investigate how many cubes in an 8 x 8 x 8 cubic board, leading to an n x n x n cube. You are not expected to investigate all these (though feel free to do so if you wish!). These suggested extensions to the original problem simply serve to indicate to you just how an initial idea can be developed up to A level and beyond.

In Chapter 6 you saw how some data-handling questions might be opened up to give children, almost incidentally, some ownership, purpose and hence motivation for learning about data handling. Similarly, the pattern spotting involved in the chessboard activity enables children to rehearse some number/algebra-related skills.

Remember too Cockcroft's (DES 1982) reference to the need for children to solve 'everyday' problems: the chessboard problem might be considered more purely mathematical than an investigation of whether those with longer legs can run faster.

Task 6

Identify the kinds of problems given to children in your school. Is there a mix of 'everyday' and mathematical? Below are several problems compiled from various sources which you might like to try yourself. If possible, choose and adapt one to try with one of your classes.

- A teacher has to deliver a message across a desert. Crossing the desert takes nine days. One teacher can carry enough food to last her 12 days. No food is available where the message must be delivered. Two teachers set out. Can the message be delivered and both teachers return to their starting point without going short of food? (Food may be buried on the way out and used on the way back.)
- Can we devise a method of helping new pupils find their way around school? Can we devise a system which will help to keep the classroom tidy?
- Use a calculator to help you with these problems:

    From 761 take 385;

    Take 139 from 482;

    I have £278. How much do I need to make £570?

- There is only one number apart from 1 which divides exactly into 163231, 152057 and 135749. What is it?
- How many trays are required, at 30lb per tray, to make up an order for 2820lb of produce?
- In two weeks' time I can order the exercise books for next year. There isn't much money so it's important that we get the right sort and the right number. This order form shows what we bought last year. Can you work out ways in which we could save money?

- A child wants to get a new bike. List the factors that she should take into account when choosing it.
- A woman has three sons. The product of the sons' ages is 200. The oldest son is twice the age of the second oldest. Find the ages of all three sons.

It is worth thinking about how you went about the task you chose, even if you didn't manage to complete it. Did you ask others? How might you rephrase these problems appropriately for a given class – could infants act out the desert problem, for instance? Which ones did you enjoy attempting and why was this?

⑤ Open-ended questions

Children will be able to develop the skills demanded of Ma1 if they are given some responsibility for their own actions and learning from the early years on. The use of open-ended questions and tasks, should be a major feature of your teaching.

Task 7

Observe a range of classrooms. Compare the number of closed and open questions given to children. Which predominate? Why do you think this might be?

Different questions encourage children to:

- recall facts
- use facts
- hypothesise or predict
- design and compare procedures
- interpret results
- apply reasoning.

Find an example for each one.

Complete the table in Figure 7.1 with your own ideas on identifying levels in Ma3.

Level	Name of Child(ren)	Activity which demonstrated attainment at this level
1		
2		
3		
4		
5		
6		

Figure 7.1 Identifying levels in Ma3

Task 8

For each set of activities in Figure 7.2, make up some open questions or directions to help children to articulate and extend their thinking. Some suggestions are offered afterwards.

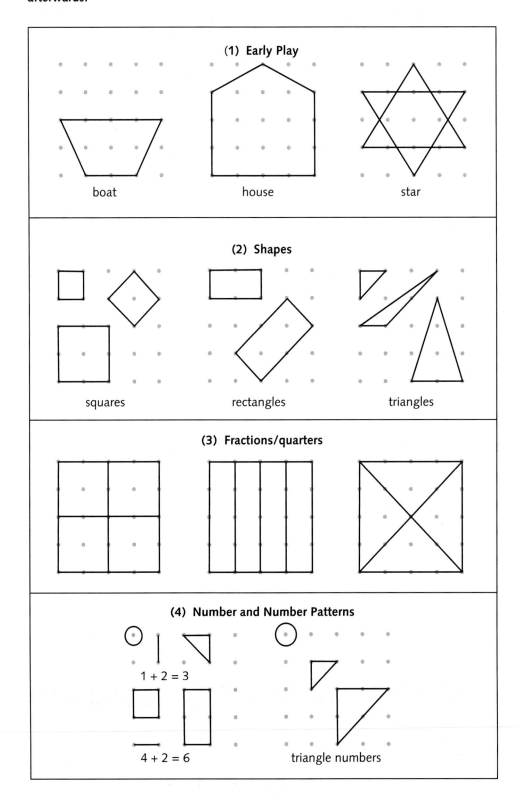

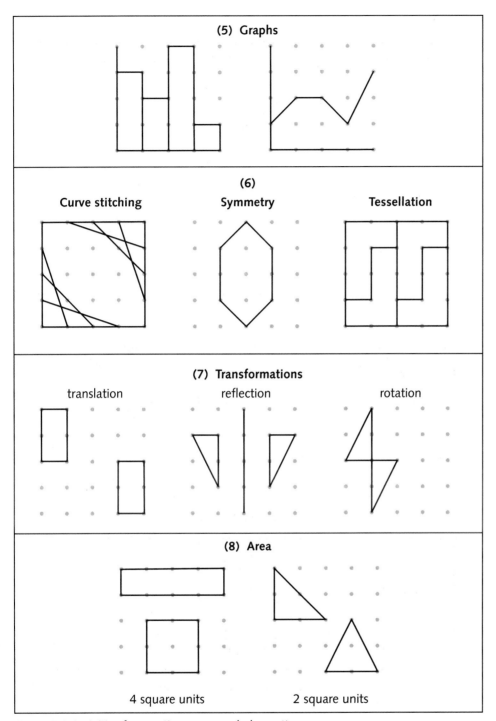

Figure 7.2 Activities for creating open-ended questions

(1) 'Come and show me what you've made. Tell me about it. Can you make a bigger smaller/longer/shorter one? How many corners/edges? Can you make one with more/ fewer corners?'

(2) 'Make as many shapes as you can. Can you tell me what they're called? Can you make a bigger/smaller shape? What does it look like if you turn your board around?'

(3) 'Split the board into quarters. Can you do it in different ways? How many? What about other fractions? Are there any you can't make? Why not?'

(4) 'Can you show me some sums? What patterns can you make with triangles?'

(5) 'Hassan has made this graph. What can you tell me from it?'

(6) 'Can you make a different curve? Make a shape with two lines of symmetry. Now another one? And again...? Can you use this "L" shape to fill your board. How many do you need? Make some more of your own.'

(7) 'Show me a translation of this rectangle. Are there any more? Make a shape and reflect it in this mirror line. What happens if I put the mirror in a different place?'

'What fraction of a turn/angle have you rotated your shape? Did you turn it clockwise or anticlockwise? What would it look like if you turned it through another angle clockwise/anticlockwise?'

(8) 'How many different shapes can you make with an area of 4, 2, $1\frac{1}{2}$, etc. squares? Can you make shapes with the same perimeter but a different area? What about same area but different perimeter?'

You may not have found this task easy, but with experience it will become less difficult. You should also be able to use and develop the above suggestions.

Can the children devise a game from the apparatus?

Task 9 (Optional)

Find how many lines of different length you can make on the 5 x 5 pinboard? Prediction?
Now find a friend and toss a coin to decide who goes first. To play:
Each player begins with 30 points and takes it in turn to place one of the lengths on the board. Points are lost when:

1. A band touches another band (lose 1 point);

2. A band cuts another band (lose 2 points);

3. A band is superimposed on another (lose 3 points).

The winner has most points left at the end.

(Note: in practice it is convenient to have an extra board with the 14 different length bands placed on it at the start of the game.)

The strands of Ma1 are based on a perception of children as active participants in learning mathematics.

Chapter 8

Planning, assessing, recording and reporting

Objectives

By the end of this chapter you will:

- understand the need for comprehensive planning;
- have a good understanding of the planning cycle, including the relationship between long-, medium- and short-term planning;
- be aware of the essential requirements of a well-planned lesson;
- be aware of some benefits of collaborative teaching in your early experience;
- understand the different purposes and natures of formative and summative assessment;
- have begun to investigate the assessment and marking approaches used in your school;
- be aware of some models of teacher assessment and recording.

① Planning

Good planning is essential as it enables you to:
- ensure that your pupils benefit from the full range of mathematical experiences;
- manage children's learning effectively;
- make informed judgements about their progress;
- fulfil statutory and local requirements.

Figure 8.1 clearly sets out the cyclic model of planning showing the interrelationships between the programme of study, attainment targets (ATs) and classroom practice.

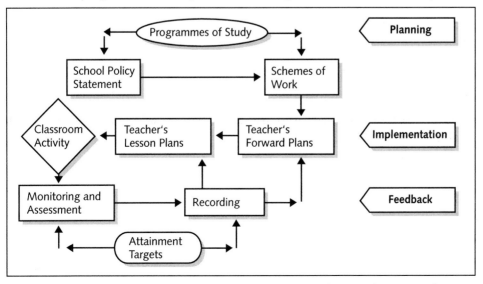

Figure 8.1 The cyclic model of planning (taken from National Curriculum Council 1989)

Figure 8.2 indicates the several contexts and levels of planning which need to take place.

Context	Outcome
Whole school	School policy statement/document on mathematics
Long term (e.g. over a key stage)	Scheme of work
Medium term (e.g. over a topic)	Forward plan
Short term	Weekly planning sheet
Daily	Lesson plans

Figure 8.2 Planning contexts and related outcomes

Individual schools will have developed their own mechanisms to implement the planning model, often with advice from their LEA and are strongly influenced by the NNS.

Task 1

Read pp. 41 and 42 of the introduction to the NNF entitled 'Principles of good planning' and refer back to Chapter 3, 'The National Numeracy Framework'. Compare a lesson plan from your first planning days as a trainee to one of your more recent ones. What are the main differences?

 Getting started in your teaching

A collaborative approach to teaching with your mentor in your early experience will support you in developing your planning skills and will give you confidence when you begin teaching on your own. At first you might use your mentor's plans to teach small groups within the class before moving on to whole-class teaching. Then your mentor might try teaching the class based on your planning. Joint evaluation of the outcomes will be a salutary experience.

Remember that all planning should be underpinned by the notion of 'fitness for purpose': the style of teaching used should be appropriate to your lesson context and aims. Exposition, the imparting of information, is only efficient if you have the attention of all the children. One (behaviourist) strategy is: 'Look at the floor, look at the wall, look at the ceiling, look at me!', then wait a few seconds, making eye contact as necessary. Compare how you might arrange classroom furniture to achieve this with the arrangement required to facilitate the practical, investigative and discussion elements of the Cockcroft Report (DES 1982), paragraph 243.

Task 2

Make a note or diagram of the furniture arrangements within different classrooms. Do they change or not? Find out why this might be.

Different groupings of both children and seating arrangements within your classroom are essential to facilitate the variety of teaching and learning techniques you will be using. Each has advantages and disadvantages. For example, while exposition and explanation to the whole class may be best served if each child is facing the teacher, this does not have to be in formal rows. A horseshoe arrangement of seating can also achieve this but has the possibility of interaction and eye contact among the children if required. If pupil-to-pupil interaction and discussion is required, perhaps if they are working collaboratively on a practical problem or investigative task, then this will be best effected in small groups. Of course, the physical characteristics of your classroom may act as a constraint, though in some open-plan rooms, for example, two teachers may be able to carry out some planned collaborative teaching. The NNS (p. 29 of the Introduction) offers further advice on this.

Task 3

How are children grouped for mathematics in your class/in the school? Many schools are now teaching year groups together in ability groups. What implications does this have for (1) teachers and for (2) children?

 Assessing, recording, reporting

You will need to be aware of the different forms of assessing and their associated purposes. In this section teacher assessment (TA) will be considered generally as the informal gathering of evidence, whether oral, aural or recorded (written, pictorial, display, electronic), collected using a variety of media (observation, discussion, questioning, formal testing) and in a range of contexts (individual, group, whole class). TA may be carried out at specified times of the year (standardised tests may be given at the beginning or end of each school year), but generally it is an ongoing or formative process. It also has a diagnostic function in its main purpose of the continuous monitoring of children's attainment to ensure that their rate of progress can be maintained or accelerated as appropriate.

By contrast, summative assessment is usually carried out at the end of some specified period of study, and is an attempt to summarise children's achievements over that time. So, for example, teachers use their formative evidence to match the most appropriate level description from the attainment targets in order to give children a numerical summary of their attainment. To ensure a 'best fit' they have to consider descriptions above and below the notional level ascribed. The marking scheme for the SATs and *Standards in Mathematics: Exemplification of Key Learning Objectives from Reception to Year 6* (QCA 1999) provide guidance for this process.

Teachers' judgements are confirmed by the numerical levels children gain in the SATs held at the end of each key stage. These too are examples of summative assessment.

A school's assessment policy for each subject, including mathematics, is usually a reflection of the overall assessment strategy set out in its policy document. The most useful documents are those which give exemplars of children's work with explanations of how a score or level was arrived at and the context in which the work was set. They should also suggest practical ways of collecting evidence.

Task 4

Read the introduction to the NNF (pp. 2–43). Identify the ways in which assessment is used in your school for planning, teaching and reporting. If possible look at reports to parents and identify the information given and key phrases used.

Marking

A related and major concern, especially for trainee teachers, is how, and how often, children's work should be marked. Questions (not just specifically for maths) which you may wish to have answered are likely to include:

- Should I mark every piece of work every day?
- Do children have to complete every example and get everything correct before they move on?
- Should the work be marked with children (individually) present?
- How do I record my mark – by drawing a 'smiley' or 'unhappy' face to signify approval or otherwise; by giving a mark out of ten (and how do I know that my seven out of ten is equivalent to another teacher's seven out of ten)?
- Are children allowed to mark and comment on their own work and how is this monitored?
- How, and where, do I record and keep my assessments?
- For how long do I need to keep my records?
- Who monitors my assessments?

Task 5

Describe or list your school's practice by adding to and answering the above questions. You may have to peruse your school's documentation carefully.

If recommended practice is modified in the classroom then seek advice and clarification from your mentor.

As part of the evaluation of your teaching you need to keep in your file selected, possibly appended, examples of children's work which you have marked and assessed, flagging up evidence of their (and your!) success. These pieces of work should always be annotated.

Homework

There are a number of different books on the market which have been developed to support homework. Your school will have a homework policy and may be using one of these published homework schemes. The NNF provides some additional guidance on out-of-class work and homework.

Chapter 9

ICT and mathematics

Objectives

By the end of this chapter you will:

- be aware of the need to review your own ICT capability and the need to address this appropriately;
- have reviewed a range of ICT devices used to teach maths in schools;
- be aware of some of the benefits and drawbacks of learning and teaching maths with ICT;
- be aware of some classroom management strategies and their implications;
- have a balanced perspective on the use of calculators, especially in a pedagogical context;
- have begun to reflect on the practice of your school;
- know the requirements of ICT within mathematics.

ICT involves more than computers

You will be aware that by the end of a teacher training course, the TTA requires that you have reviewed and demonstrated your own knowledge, skills and understanding of ICT, as well as being competent in using it appropriately to teach, in this case, mathematics. You may, for example, have little, if any, experience of LOGO. Although ICT connotations are predominantly computer-related you must also remember that they do include the use of video and audio resources, as well as the calculator. (Source: DfEE: Circular 4/98 Annex B.)

Task 1

Use a television listings journal to identify current maths television programmes for schools. Are any of these used in your school? If so, how do they fit into the curriculum? If not, why might this be?

You will find a wealth of maths-specific TV series aimed at a whole range of children, not including 'generic' programmes such as *Sesame Street*. One of their major benefits is that they can take maths out of the classroom, showing novel and stimulating contexts for the maths being learned. Schools may record selected series (or borrow them from LEA resource centres) and build them into their maths curriculum. If they are not used there may be pragmatic reasons for this. If you can, watch an appropriate series – they usually come with documented resources and ideas which you might be able to integrate into your teaching, even if you do not use the recordings.

ICT and computers

Most work in ICT will, however, be focused on computers, and their potential for helping children to learn maths.

Task 2

Think about and list the ways that computers can help children to learn maths. Are there any negative aspects?

Negative aspects usually relate to the difficulty of access for children, especially in terms of the numbers of computers available and the management implications of this. Teachers' unfamiliarity with both hardware and software may be another contributory factor. (It is useful here to distinguish between 'small software' such as puzzles and adventure games, which is dedicated to enriching specific areas of the maths curriculum; 'drill and practice' programs which often reproduce routine algorithms; and 'generic' software, such as spreadsheets and data-handling packages, which may be used across a range of mathematics and other subjects.)

Another important issue is that your teaching objectives must be clear. Do you want the children to use ICT to learn some maths, or is the maths a convenient context for them to learn ICT? Is the extended time and effort they need to master a piece of unfamiliar software worth the intended gain in mathematics understanding?

Positive aspects include rapid, accurate and non-judgemental feedback to the child, for example, seeing the overall effect of changing one or more numbers or conditions. ICT can also remove the tedium of written routines, and gives the ability to generate many examples. This latter allows the possibility of children seeing underlying patterns, generalising these into conjectures (hypotheses) and predictions, and testing them – thus fulfilling many of the requirements of Ma1 and, particularly, the algebra subsection of Ma2. In Chapter 6 (for Ma4) it has been indicated that ICT can facilitate work with large amounts of real, rather than contrived, data. For Ma3, ICT can show geometric relationships more clearly by making it easier to manipulate visual images and shapes.

Task 3

Throughout the course you will need to familiarise yourself with ICT and try to use it in your teaching. Make a list of the software used in your class, familiarise yourself with it and classify it into the National Curriculum sections.

The NCET (National Council for Educational Technology) (1997) leaflet, *Primary Maths with IT*, summarises and provides examples of how IT can make a significant contribution towards the teaching and learning of maths in five areas, particularly by using '**generic**' software.

More specifically, spreadsheets are a powerful tool in mathematics and have functions appropriate for children at all key stages. Numbers do not have to be entered in an organised way, the spreadsheet can sort them as required later. Its graphing facility can be used to represent pairs of numbers and give a picture of relationships between them. For example, plotting sets of equivalent fractions such as $\frac{1}{2}, \frac{2}{4}, \frac{3}{6}, \frac{4}{8}$, etc. as coordinate pairs, gives straight lines of varying steepness and hence offers another way of comparing the size of fractions. From this children may begin to generalise and conjecture that the larger the denominator, the smaller the fraction (for a constant numerator) and test this with other fractions.

3 LOGO

LOGO may be the most unfamiliar part of ICT to you. Essentially, it enables children to use a simple programming language to move a screen turtle in exploring the dynamics of shape and space and number relationships. It is usually developed from very young children's experiences of using a similar language to programme a floor toy (often a ROAMER). The act of writing a sequenced set of instructions (or procedures) to make the turtle follow a predetermined path, with instant feedback of the result, can help children to develop a logical approach to problem solving. The evidence on the screen can help you to make informal assessments.

Task 4

If you have not already done so, make sure that you are familiar with ROAMER and whichever version of LOGO is used with your classes.

4 Calculators

Calculators, currently the most portable and widely-available piece of ICT hardware, were described in Chapter 1 as having the potential to be used as a pedagogical or teaching resource, especially for exploring our number system. For example, with discussion calculators can support early ideas of counting and the four arithmetic operations. Children may use a calculator as a checking device as they bounce along the number line in steps of different or the same size. By doing this counting, numbers are extended to include negative numbers quite naturally.

One of the arguments given against children using calculators for computation is that they often employ them in a mindless and trivial way, accepting whatever answer is displayed, and using them for calculations which could be done quicker mentally. This would seem to indicate that they are not interacting with, nor even particularly interested in, their mathematics. If this is the case, then it would seem right to examine just what mathematical experiences such children are being given. However, even when children use them for 'just' calculating there are still opportunities for them to exhibit and practise their knowledge, skills and understanding. In particular these include checking mechanisms such as (implicitly) using the commutative law to perform a multiplication or addition in a different order and comparing the results for agreement; changing the numbers to equivalent forms and performing the operation(s); rounding numbers to some convenient approximation and estimating with these to check whether the calculated result is of the right order of size.

Task 5

Identify the place of calculators in your school. Are they freely available? Are there enough? How does practice compare with policy? Ask the children how many of them use calculators at home.

Ideas about place value especially can be reinforced using the calculator and help to eradicate misconceptions and half truths such as 'to multiply by ten add a nought on the end'. Try the following activities for yourself.

Enter any number into your calculator.

Multiply it by 10, repeat, repeat, ...

What do you notice? (*The digits move one place to the left.*)

Can you predict what might happen if you use other numbers?

Try it and see.

Were you right?

Well done!

What do you think might happen if you multiply by 100?

Try it and see.

Does it work with other numbers?

Well done!

If you entered 3.4 what would you get?

Can you think what I'm going to ask you now? (*Multiply by 1000.*)

Yes! What would be the answer to 6.7 x 1000? (*6700.*)

Do you need to check it on the calculator? (*No, but does so!*)

So, finally can you tell me a way of multiplying by powers of ten without using the calculator? (Does so and records the 'rule'.)

Now repeat the process but this time divide by 0.1, 0.01, 0.001, and so on.

Tell me what you've found. (*x10 and ÷0.1 are equivalent operations.*)

Now predict and test a rule for dividing by ten, a hundred, and so on.

Compare this with multiplying your numbers by 0.1, 0.01, 0.001, etc.

Tell me what you've found. (*÷10 and x0.1 are equivalent operations.*)

Basic place value ideas can be reinforced by using the 'Place Invaders' game:

The basic game

Enter any 3-digit number into a calculator. Each digit is an 'alien'. To get rid of these aliens you have to eliminate them individually by subtracting from each digit in turn, starting from the units position to leave zero. For example:

354 – 4	leaves	
350 – 50	leaves	(Some children will subtract 5 and get a shock!)
300 – 300	leaves	
0	aliens gone!	

The game can be differentiated to suit the current attainment of individuals.

You could:

- increase or decrease the number of digits;
- eliminate digits in order of size (first the 3(00), followed by the 4, then the 5(0)), or in the reverse order;
- use decimal fractions and repeat the two approaches above;
- only allow digits to be eliminated if they are in the units position (which means practising and reinforcing multiplying and dividing by 10, 100, etc.);
- change digits to zero by adding. (For this version the final calculator display will begin with a 1.)

In Chapter 4 it was mentioned how some children were unaware of the infinite nature of decimals. The calculator can be used, with a number line, to model the results, helping children to understand this while simultaneously practising a **bisection** technique. This is the process of continuing to halve the difference between two numbers until a number of appropriate degree of accuracy is obtained.

- Enter 27 into your display.
- Find me a number to multiply this by to get 100 in the display.
- *4 is too big. 3 is too small. Let's try halfway. How do I enter $3\frac{1}{2}$?*
- Does anybody know? Try 3.5. *Still too small.*
- And so on.

Children need encouragement to record their multiplying number each time. At the end their findings and strategies are summarised. 'Is it possible to get exactly 100?' If they haven't thought of it for themselves you could tell them that a quicker way would be to divide 100 by 27. But this would spoil the point of the exercise!

The same activity can be done as a game called 'Squeeze' (there are other names for it).
- I'm thinking of a number between 1 and 100. (Choose a range to suit the current attainments of the children.)
- I want you to tell me what it is.
- I can only answer yes or no to your questions.

'Is it bigger/smaller than 50?' would be a good first question to ask as it cuts down the number of possibilities. What question would you ask next? And so on.

Some children may ask if it is odd. If the answer is no then they can assume it is even (unless of course you've chosen a decimal fraction! Only whole numbers are odd or even. If the children don't realise this the first time they come across it they certainly do the next!).

Of course these activities can be carried out without a calculator and most children would not find them a problem. However, for reasons outlined above, especially that of the ICT device being non-judgemental, a calculator can support less confident children who perhaps need extra time to reflect and fix ideas in their minds.

5 The benefits of ICT

Earlier in this chapter it was suggested that pragmatic considerations may lead to a reluctance to use ICT in classrooms. It is therefore worth looking at the benefits of some classroom management techniques to cater for a variety of contexts.

(a) Whole-class single screen:
The only reasonably-sized screen that most primary schools have is the one usually used with an OHP. However, use of this enables the teacher to monitor the class and ask 'What if...?' or 'What happens next...? questions before the next prepared image is displayed.

(b) Small group-circus:
A number of activities, generally focused on the same theme, are set out around the classroom. Each group, in turn, completes an activity before moving on to the next. The benefits of this approach are that children are involved in a range of learning experiences, it provides equal access to all and maximises the use of resources. The major drawback is that groups work at different rates, may become more or less involved in one activity and, unless an 'overflow' activity is provided, some children may lose valuable time waiting for their turn, even failing to complete all the activities.

(c) Individual or pairs – independent:
As there are generally only a few machines in the classroom, children may be given time out from the major class activity to use a particular piece of apparatus or software which is seen as essential to their learning, but which may or may not be related to the class-focused topic. One strategy within this is peer teaching, where one 'expert' child teaches another how to use the apparatus or software. This new expert then passes on his or her knowledge in the same way until the whole class has been taught. The danger with this is that unless it is carefully monitored and reviewed, by the time all children have become expert any knowledge and expertise gained may have been forgotten or become fragmented.

(d) Pairs – independent:
If your school is fortunate enough to have access to a large number (a class set!) of computers then some of the problems above become minimised, though perhaps not minimal! Pairings of children at one machine enable mutual support to be given

and expertise to be shared. Discussion between pairs may be supplemented and extended by discussion with other pairs on either side. If children are all working on the same software then joint findings can be reviewed. If they are using different software then alternative perspectives can be articulated and presented. However, it is well to be aware that the use of ICT has implications for your teaching. Normally it would be you, the teacher, who provides the feedback, but the computer allows you, much more, to work alongside the children. In this way a less formal, but more accurate assessment of their knowledge, skills and understanding can be made.

Central Government Training Pack
At the end of 2000, schools were sent a training pack entitled *Using ICT to support mathematics in primary schools* (DfEE 2000a). This is a very useful and practical resource. It aims to:
• Clarify when, when not, and how to use ICT to support the teaching of mathematics.
• Focus the use of ICT in mathematics on objectives from the NNF.
• Suggest useful starting points for teaching.
• Show teachers how to use small programs to support their teaching and children's learning of mathematics.
Trainee teachers will find the Video cassette, CD-ROM, Software user guide, Handling data booklet and the 14 Sample lessons most useful.
Video sequence 1 is particularly helpful in identifying the range of ICT used to support mathematics. It helps remind us all that ICT is much more than using computer.

Uses in the video include:
• Taking pictures of shapes with a digital camera.
• Using a floor robot to move along a path.
• Researching data from a CD-ROM encyclopedia.
• Using pocket calculators for fractions and decimals.
• Listening to audio tapes for learning counting and multiplication facts.
• Using computer programs for number with a large screen monitor and projector.
• Using a 'binary tree' computer program to sort a set of numbers.
• Watching a television broadcast about multiplication.
• Collecting data from the Internet about the weather.
• Using an electronic whiteboard to demonstrate number patterns.
• Using a video camera to record birds visiting a bird table.
• Using a sensor attached to the computer to gather data over a period of time.
• Using a computer film to explore shapes.
• Using an overhead calculator for fractions and decimals.

Task 6
Read the section on ICT in the NNS (p. 31 of the Introduction).
Identify how ICT, particularly the use of computers, is managed in your school. To what extent does practice match policy? If other models of classroom organisation are used list them, and explain their benefits and drawbacks.

Task 7
Find the units of work in the QCA/DfEE (1998) (Updated 2000) *Information technology*. Look at what a particular year group in your key stage should cover. Photocopy this and highlight those sections which are likely to be covered in mathematics.

Task 8
Finally, return to Figure 1.1 on p. 5 where you were asked to locate your current feelings towards maths. Mark in a new point if you think your view has changed. Explain why this is. Even if there's been no change explain why.

Chapter 10

References and further reading

ATM (1985) *Notes on Mathematics for Children*. Derby: ATM.

Cooke, H. (2001) *Passport to Professional Numeracy*. London: David Fulton Publishers.

Deboys, M. and Pitt, E. (1993) *Lines of development in primary mathematics*. Belfast: Blackstaff Press.

DES (1982) *Mathematics Counts* (Cockcroft Report). London: HMSO.

DfEE (1998) Circular 4/98: *Teaching: High Status: High Standards*. London: DfEE.

DfEE (1999a) *The National Numeracy Strategy: Framework for Teaching Mathematics from Reception to Year 6*. London: DfEE.

DfEE (1999b) *Three-day course tutor's pack* (includes Numeracy Video). London: DfEE.

DfEE (1999c) *National Numeracy Strategy Mathematical Vocabulary*. London: DfEE.

DfEE (2000a) *Using ICT to support mathematics in primary schools*. (Ref: DfEE 026/2000). London: DfEE.

DfEE (2000b) *Curriculum Guidance for the foundation stage*. London: DfEE.

DfEE/QCA (1999) *The National Curriculum 2000*. London: HMSO.

Fielker, D. (1996) 'Turn the tables on chanting' in *TES Extra* (4th October 1996).

Fleet, T. and Fleet E. (1997) *Maths homework series*. Bedfordshire: Belair Publications.

Fuson, K. C. and Kwon, Y. (1991) 'Chinese-based regular and European irregular systems of number words: The disadvantages for English-speaking children' (2nd edn), in Durkin, K. and Shire, B. (1991) ibid.

Haylock, D. (2001) *Mathematics Explained for Primary Teachers* (2nd edn). London: Paul Chapman Publishing.

Jennings, S. and Dunne, R. (1997) *Mathematics for Primary Teachers: An audit and self-study guide*. London: Letts Educational.

Liebeck, P. (1990) *How Children Learn Mathematics: A Guide for Parents and Teachers*. London: Penguin.

Mooney, C. *et al.* (2000) *Primary Mathematics: Knowledge and Understanding*. Exeter: Learning Matters.

NCET (1997) *Primary Maths with IT*. Coventry: NCET.

Open University (1992) *E242 Learning for All: Unit 6/7: Classroom Diversity*, pp. 67–8. Milton Keynes: OU.

Open University (1996) *Mathematics: Primary Module 2: Teaching in primary schools*. Milton Keynes: OU.

Open University (1998) *M521 Passport to Mathematics*. Milton Keynes: OU.

Pinel, A. (1992) 'Unwinding the Strands', *Strategies* **2** (3), pp. 14–5.

Plunkett, S. (1977) 'Decomposition and All that Rot', in ATM and MA (eds) *Calculators in the Primary School*. London: ATM.

QCA (1999) *Standards in Mathematics: Exemplification of Key Learning Objectives from Reception to Year 6*. London: QCA.

QCA/DfEE (1998) (Updated 2000) *Information technology*. London: QCA.

QCA/DfEE (2000) *Curriculum Guidance for the foundation stage*. London: QCA.

Skemp, R. (1979) 'Relational understanding and instrumental understanding', in *Mathematics Teaching* **77**.

Suggate, J. *et al.* (2001) *Mathematical Knowledge for Primary Teachers*, 2nd Edn. London: David Fulton Publishers.

TTA (1999) Assessing your needs in literacy, mathematics, science: Needs assessment materials (CD-ROM). London: TTA.

Useful websites

These tend to date very quickly. Government sites such as the DfEE standards site and the TTA site are up-dated regularly and have good links to relevant sites.
DfEE standards site: www.standards.dfee.gov.uk
TTA site: www.teach-tta.gov.uk
TTA publications list: www.canteach.gov.uk

Internet sites for maths education (accessed May 2001)
1. **Maths Den:** *www.actden.com*
    Upper Key Stage 2.
    For children and teachers who want a challenging maths problem to solve. Problem posed every week, these can be used as extension work or tests. There is a search facility which lets you find problems on specific topics. It gives tips on how to solve the problems, you can send in your answers, enter competitions and link to other maths educational sites. Appealing graphics.
2. **Mega Math:** *www.c3.lanl.gov/mega-math/*
    Upper Key Stage 2.
    This is a resource site for teachers. It gives very good definitions of mathematical language, and has very good graphics which are used to illustrate points. This page has problems which can be simplified for the children to tackle. It is easy to move around this site.
3. **BBC Education:** *www.bbc.co.uk/education*
    Hard to find your way around. All key stages, but unclear labelling, as all the sites have numbers. Index needed, though the authors haven't found this yet. This site looks promising to start with as the front page graphics are good but it soon deteriorates. This site is not recommended unless you have a lot of time on your hands.
4. **Puzzle ring:** *www.geocities.com/WestHollywood/2555/puzzling.html*
    Innovative. Maths puzzles for all ages. You can add puzzles, take puzzles off, send off your answers. New puzzle every two weeks. It can be used as part of a mental maths programme in the school. It has a handy search facility but no answer page.
5. **IBM Maths Site:** *www.solutions.ibm.com/k12/teacher/96jul.html*
    Useful for teachers and pupils. Key Stages 1, 2, 3, 4 and 5. Specified weekly topics which are studied in depth. Large archive section. Site divided into 4 sections: teacher activities, pupil activities, downloading resources and educational links. The graphics are exciting, and the quality of work on the site is challenging.
6. **IBM Maths Forum:** *www.forum.swarthmore.edu/*
    Linking site to maths education and resources for both teachers and children for all age ranges and most topics. Easy to find your way around, the resources are kept up-to-date. This site is useful both for teachers and students who want to find out more about a topic. Each topic contains lesson plans, problems and resources.

7. **Flashcards:** *www.edu4kids.com/math/*
   Key Stage 1 number. An interactive site which lets you test the accuracy of addition and subtraction skills. You can set the level and then the site will test the children with a series of quick-fire problems. The responses are timed and there is a breakdown at the end so that you can assess the strengths and weaknesses of the child.

8. **Beat the Calculator:** *www.forum.swarthmore.edu/k12/mathtips/beatcalc.html*
   Key Stage 2 number. A test page on which you can choose the type of maths you wish to do and you are given a problem which you have to solve before the calculator. This site is good for building up mental maths capacities, as well as the speed and accuracy of calculations.

9. **Clever games for clever people:**
   www.cs.uidaho.edu/~casey931/conway/games.html
   Upper Key Stage 2 number. A collection of different games based on similar boards. These can be used either as assessment or as introductory activities. The single drawback is that you have to look at the site first to see whether you have the correct material to play the game.

10. **Monster math:** *www.lifelong.com/k12/maths.asp*
    Lower Key Stage 2/Upper Key Stage 1, number and Using and Applying. This is designed to introduce and review a variety of basic mathematic concepts such as counting, addition and multiplication. It is written in a variety of different languages so that it can be used all over the world. This site has brilliant graphics and is loads of fun.

Index